COINS
and
COIN COLLECTING

COINS
and
COIN COLLECTING

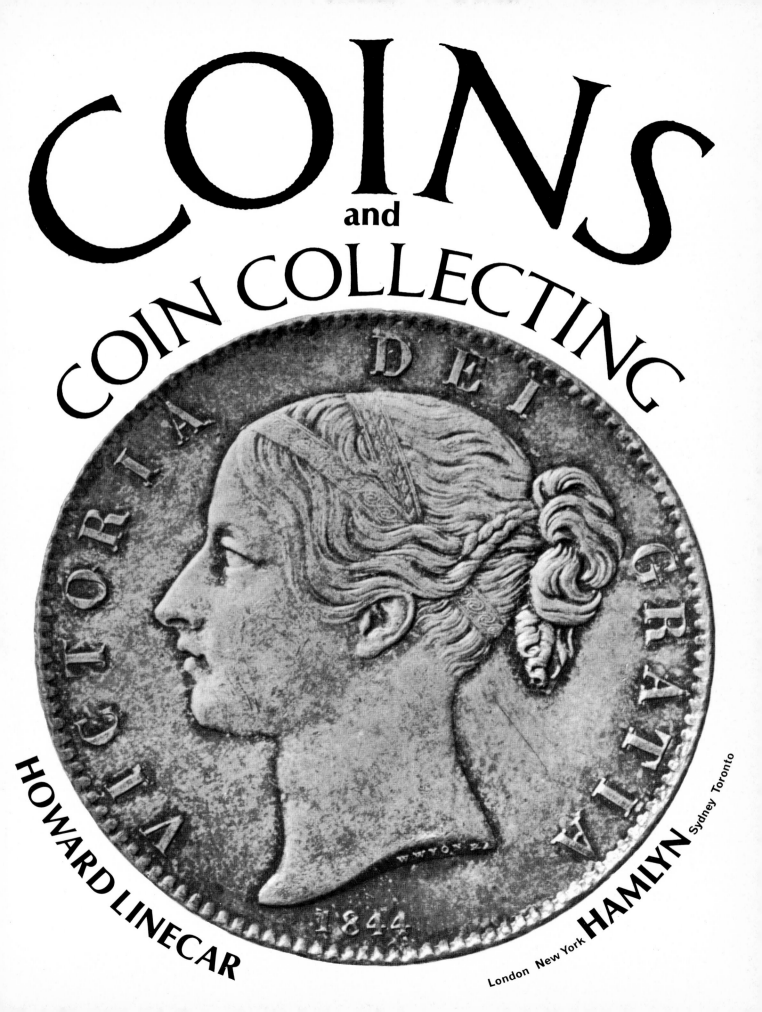

HOWARD LINECAR

London New York **HAMLYN** Sydney Toronto

Jacket illustration:
New British 50 Penny Piece
Australian Florin
Victoria 'Gothic' Crown
George III Twopence
Spanish 8 Reale
Edward VI gold Sovereign
Syracuse silver Decadrachm
USA Double Eagle

Front endpaper:
Attic Tetradrachm
Trajan on a Sestertius

Half-title page:
Francis I silver Testoon
Elizabeth I Half-pound piece

Title page and back endpaper:
USA Broken Dollar
Victoria 'Young head' Crown

Published by
The Hamlyn Publishing Group Ltd
London New York Sydney Toronto
Hamlyn House The Centre Feltham
Middlesex
© Copyright The Hamlyn Publishing Group
Ltd 1971

ISBN 0 600 31605 X

Filmset by Photoprint Plates Ltd., Rayleigh,
Essex

Printed in Italy by Arnoldo Mondadori
Editore Verona

CONTENTS

COLLECTING COINS

Though the interest in coin collecting has grown rapidly in the last twenty years, it is by no means a new form of study. The present interest has been brought about by a number of factors. Many countries, particularly those within, or once within, the British Commonwealth of Nations, have for various reasons decided to place their currency on a decimal basis. Almost the last among them is Britain, which will be using its familiar series of coins for the last time not long after this book is published. These words are being written three days after the Halfpenny ceased to be legal tender. The Farthing was demonetized on 1 January 1961 and the Halfcrown has disappeared. A large number of people, therefore, are taking an interest in the disappearing denominations (partly in the hope of making a profit out of their collection in the years to come) both in Britain and in other countries which have already made the change; Australia and New Zealand, for example.

A further reason for the greater interest in coin collecting is the high rate of taxation in many countries and a lack of trust in more usual forms of investment. Investors and collectors have put their money into coins—as into pictures, books, silver and various other objects of art and value.

Many of the newly created countries and many of the older countries, seeing a market offered, have produced limited issues of their new or old established coinages and sold them at premium price. These have been readily taken up and in the main have proved a good investment.

The type of collector mentioned so far is more of an investor than a student of coin collecting. Many such investor-collectors eventually turn into student-collectors and therefore become numismatists.

The numismatist—the student-collector of coins as well as the professional numismatist charged with the keeping of coin collections in the major museums of the world—has been active for many hundreds of years—even since Roman times, when there were not so many coins to collect as there are now. In Britain and Europe collecting became fashionable and led to serious numismatic studies in about the seventeenth and eighteenth centuries.

This, in part, led to the foundation of many of the major public collections, now housed in museums. Many of the great collectors of the past donated the whole or part of their collections. Others passed their collections on to their descendants. Some of these collections exist today and several are still being increased. The great museum collections are also continually growing through donations and purchases.

Collections, great and small, are constantly being broken up. They may be sold at auction, where numerous coins thus pass to other collections, or they may be sold to coin dealers, who distribute them among their many customers, including the museums.

Coin collecting, then, is, and has been for centuries, a live and active science, study and hobby. The collector, student or investor, who comes newly to the scene is taking a part in an ancient and important science. What he collects, how he uses his collection and what ultimately happens to it, is important to the coin collecting picture as a whole.

Practically every collector starts for some slightly different reason. In the present coin-collecting world collectors tend to fall into two broad classes, the student-collector and the investor-collector. The latter is primarily out to make a profitable investment, and therefore studies the long list of coins issued by the dealers who specialize in catering for his needs and who exist by making money out of his investments.

The student-collector usually starts his collection through personal choice. He may be interested in history, art or archaeology; some coin or type of coin, such as a Crown size piece, may appeal to him. He may have been given or left a few coins, or he may have found some in an old forgotten box. Something about them fires his imagination. He decides to follow up some thought, some line of inquiry, some collecting theme. Once he has started, or is about to start, certain basic advice can be offered for his consideration.

There are two main sources of supply that are open to him. He may acquire his coins from dealers or he may buy them for himself, from auction sales or from what he sees offered by general antique dealers who do not specialize in coins. The true coin dealer's customers, whether student- or investor-collector, are his bread and butter, and he must therefore study their wants. As a theme of collecting emerges in the collector's interests, his dealer will study this theme and be on the look-out for coins which the collector needs.

If, as so often happens, an established dealer is financially strong enough to be able to buy a whole collection of coins, he at once looks at it from the point of view of the various collectors whose collections he is helping to build. He knows that Mr A wants this particular coin, or series of coins, which will fit into his collecting theme. He therefore offers them to Mr A. It is of no particular consequence if Mr A is close at hand, and can call on his dealer to look at the coins offered, or if he is in Australia—either way Mr A will

be offered the coins and, if he is a customer of standing, the dealer will probably have them sent on approval. The dealer cannot exist by accumulating a vast stock of coins. He must turn them over—break up the collection he has bought—and the 'bits and pieces' left over go into his general stock of coins only after his numerous collectors have been offered the pieces he knows they need.

The dealer attends coin auction sales in any part of the world, either personally or through his accredited agent. In coin auction catalogues important pieces are offered as single specimens. The more common coins are offered in numerically larger lots. The established dealer will advise his various customers that one or more coins which they need are being offered. He will accept bids on such coins and buy them for the collector for a commission, usually of five per cent. He will advise the collector how much a certain desired coin can be expected to realize at the sale if the collector is in doubt as to how much he should pay. The dealer will probably see that the collector has a copy of the catalogue to mull over for himself. Dealers maintain a card index of collectors to whom they send coin auction catalogues.

With the more common coins, catalogued in bulk, the dealer will frequently buy such a lot and from it offer his collectors the specimens they need, while absorbing those left over into his general stock.

If at all possible, the dealer makes personal contact with his collectors, from whatever part of the world they may come. Failing this the dealer writes personal letters to his serious collectors, each coming to know and trust the other through the mail. Only thus, by trust on both sides, can the dealer hope to survive.

Whether buying mainly from a dealer or not, the collector may

1, 2, 3 *Three of Britain's familiar coins that disappeared from circulation with the approach of Decimal Day (15 February 1971).*

decide on occasion, or as normal practice, to 'go it alone', to attend coin auction sales in person or to send his commissions to the auctioneer. This is fine, but the collector is now opposed to the ranks of coin dealers, who are probably armed with many commissions on behalf of other collectors. To 'go it alone' can therefore be expensive, since the individual buyer must bid the dealers out of the sale.

This is not to suggest that the whole business of coin collecting should be carried on through the various dealers. Competition is healthy. The dealers at the sale may have no customers interested in just that one coin or collection which the individual collector intends to buy. But the individual buyer does run the risk of paying a little more than the coin is worth. To buy against the dealers the individual must either have a sound knowledge of values of the coins in his theme of collecting; or not really be worried by any price he may have to pay—setting the pleasure of possession above the cost.

It is interesting to note that in auction sales in Britain there is no sales tax. In Europe, in particular, various governments have imposed such a tax. Thus if the collector, buying for himself or through his dealer, pays £x for a coin, he does not, in Britain, also have to pay £y sales tax. In most European countries £y can be as much as twenty per cent of the sale price. If in these European countries the collector is buying through his dealer, five or ten per cent may be the dealer's commission, but to this must be added £y government tax.

The collector may like to shop around among the coin dealers, antique dealers, antique hyper-markets and the like, in the hope of picking up a bargain here and there. Once again, to do this the collector must be armed with a sound knowledge of the value of the coins he needs. Nowadays too many coins are being offered by dealers who have come into the coin market simply to cash in on the present rise in collectors' interest. Such dealers have little of the specialized knowledge of the true coin dealer. This is no shame to them: they have their living to make. But, lacking the specialized knowledge of coin values in his own collecting theme,

the less knowledgeable collector who shops around may burn his fingers in the long run. With knowledge of the values of the coins he may equally obtain a few bargains but the possibility becomes daily more remote in face of the many published lists of coin values.

Once the collector has started to collect he must think about the housing and general maintenance of his collection. For those collectors who are interested mainly in modern coins, albums and folders are offered in which they may be housed. Basically the various types of coin albums consist of pages made of transparent plastic material, each page fitted with a number of pockets into which coins may be placed. The pages are contained in some form of binder—usually in book form—so that the binder will fit into a bookshelf.

The many folders offered usually provide housing for one special type of coin. For example the collector of British Pennies since 1860, or of United States One Cent pieces, or Canadian Five Cent pieces, is offered cardboard folders in which a hole has been punched to receive coins of consecutive dates in the series. Each hole has the date of the coin which it is designed to house stamped below it. The collector can thus see which dates he still needs in his series. Such folders may consist of a number of pages.

Both the album and the folder are excellent in their own way. They provide housing for relatively modern coins. But once the collector starts to trace back the history of some denomination, albums and folders fail to satisfy his coin housing needs. He now requires a custom-built coin cabinet in which to keep his collection.

Coin cabinets are available new and secondhand, in various shapes and sizes. As a type they usually consist of a main mahogany cabinet, fitted with runners into which slide the trays which hold the coins. The trays themselves are about half an inch thick and are pierced with circular holes to take the coins. It is usual to confine the piercings in any one tray to one particular size. One tray may take Crown pieces, the next Florins or Halfcrowns, the next Shilling size coins, and so forth. The trays are usually interchangeable within the cabinet.

4 *Many coinage designs were put forward when New Zealand changed to decimal currency in 1967.*

5 *The final choice, now in circulation.*

The collector should therefore consider the type of coins he is collecting before he buys his cabinet. If his whole collection is of coins no larger than the British Shilling it is a waste of space to buy a cabinet that will also take a large number of Crowns. Obviously the reverse is not the case. A small coin will fit, wastefully, into a large piercing but a large coin will not go into a space smaller than itself.

Most cabinets are pierced to take a general collection, but a little searching will usually produce a cabinet suitable for a specialized collection. Alternatively, if the cabinet is being made to order, the sizes of the piercings can be stated to suit the collector's requirements.

Good coin cabinets have a small hole cut through the base of the larger piercing, so that a coin can be pushed up from below with the tip of a finger. A coin stuck in a hole can easily be damaged by being dug out with a sharp pointed instrument such as a penknife blade. Each piercing is fitted with a disc of felt, similar in texture to that on a billiard table. This prevents the coin from harsh contact with the wood of the tray.

The wood of which the cabinet is made is highly important.

Experience shows that mahogany is by far the best. It is strong, so that the trays do not break under their load—coins are heavy objects in bulk—it is dry, not heavy with natural oils which will damage coins, and it does not warp if properly dried and seasoned. A tray which jams in the runners is a constant irritation and may lead to coin damage if the coins jump about when the tray is being forced in or out.

Experience has also shown that coin cabinets are best made by the expert who specializes in them. Special tools are needed to make the piercings correctly. The amateur generally runs into trouble with broken trays and roughly finished piercings.

A good convenient size is about a foot or eighteen inches cube. A cabinet of this size is not usually too heavy to be moved when filled with coins. Custom-built cabinets can be made to any required size and, if necessary, built into a room as a piece of fitted furniture—such a size, of course, is needed only by the collector on a grand scale. Locking doors should be provided.

Alternatively a carcass and trays can be made to order to fit any size of commercial safe. Coin collections are too valuable to be left lying about. If the cabinet cannot be moved for safe-keeping during absence it should be a safe in its own right.

Having decided the most suitable method of housing a collection—which may change from folder to album to cabinet as the collection grows—a little thought should be given to the actual care and maintenance of the collection itself, and in particular to the cleaning of coins.

Cleaning gold coins
Gold coins seldom get really dirty. The metal tones with age, often to a true 'old gold' colour, and this is most attractive. If a gold coin is really dirty, through being buried, it can be cleaned with mild acid, such as lemon juice. This should be applied with a pad of cotton wool: nothing rougher should ever be used. A very soft brush, such as those used professionally for cleaning silver, can then be applied to bring up the tone. A harder brush, or one made of plastic fibre bristles, should never be used. Such materials

6 *Coin cabinets at the Bibliothèque Nationale, Paris, which houses the largest numismatic collection in France.*

are quite unyielding and will scratch the coin. Gold is a soft metal and gold coins are usually only slightly alloyed to stiffen them. Though gold is not attacked by acid, a strong acid may attack the small amount of alloy in the coin and leave it pitted.

Cleaning silver coins

This is more tricky. Silver tarnishes and can go quite black. Never use any form of 'metal polish', silver polish or similar materials. These deposit a form of dust, usually white, in the tiny parts of the coin design and in particular in the lettering, and is most difficult to get rid of. Soap and warm water followed by a thorough drying on a soft towel will usually remove the worst of the dirt. It will not remove the white deposit of metal polish. Afterwards a little light breath on the coin and a gentle brushing with a silver brush will often produce a nice tone. An antique silver coin does not have to look as bright and shiny as an article of domestic silver.

Cleaning cupro-nickel coins

Modern cupro-nickel coins are much harder than silver and do not tarnish so readily. Many so-called nickel coins contain a copper or other alloy, so the same remark applies. In general, proceed as with silver coins. An unmarked cupro-nickel coin will be scratched if roughly treated.

A collector may come across coins struck in aluminium, steel (coated or otherwise), iron or zinc emergency issues, and brass and lead pieces. Aluminium does not tarnish very easily and can be treated much the same as silver. Unplated steel and iron coins can go rusty and not much can be done about it. Zinc and lead can accumulate verdigris and again not much can be done.

Cleaning copper and bronze coins

In one word, don't. If really in trouble with coins of these metals, such as with coins in a hoard dug up from the ground, or with really dirty pieces, expert advice should be sought.

In general coins should be treated as gently as possible. Don't drop them or let them knock together. Don't rub the fingers over them, breath tobacco smoke over them, or

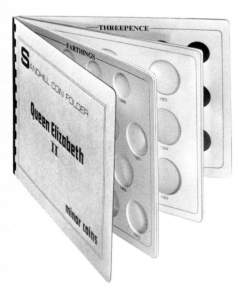

7 *Collector's coin folder—each space is reserved for a particular coin in a series.*

wrap them up in newspaper or other damp material. If bought as an investment, as 'new issues' and stored in a safe or bank vault, go and look at them from time to time. See that they are not deteriorating in a damp or humid atmosphere.

All this may sound like taking matters to extremes, but a fine coin can easily be damaged even though it is only a chunk of metal. You have paid good money for your coins, either as a student- or an investor-collector. Look after them.

When considering how to start a collection, remember this is not just a simple matter of going out and buying coins. Random selection of just anything and everything that looks like a coin is not coin collecting. Coin collecting must have a purpose and an object, especially to the student-collector. Student-collector is not really an off-putting title. Some of the world's greatest student-collectors have started to collect coins in the most humble way. The following story may not be factually one hundred per cent correct but it is not far out—it demonstrates how a student-collector may be born.

Before the First World War, in about 1902, there was a man named Valentine, a carpenter employed by the London County Council on work connected with its tramway system. Somehow he acquired a selection of what are roughly described as 'Indian' coins, the issues of the Muhammadan States and of the Indian sub-continent. Most of us shudder at these indecipherable pieces, rough and chunky, with incomprehensible legends. Not so our carpenter.

He set himself the task of understanding these coins which had caught his interest. In the preface to a book—one of four which he laboriously wrote in clear writing and which were afterwards photographed, page by page, and produced exactly as they were written—he states: 'This book was called into being through my inability to ascribe the small coin figured on the title page. For this purpose I visited the Medal Room at the British Museum, thinking to locate the mint and ruler with very little trouble, but to my surprise found it by no means an easy task. Every facility was granted me by the sympathetic custodians to enable

me to compare my coin with other coins and various engravings, but all to no purpose. Many numismatic friends, too, from time to time have seen it but the attribution of the little coin up to the present remains an unsolved problem and must remain so until a similar one comes to light bearing the missing part of the inscription. During this period I was most forcibly struck with the meagre amount of information published on Muhammadan copper coins and the still smaller number of engravings of them.

'Two of the Oriental catalogues of the British Museum certainly touched on this subject but they are almost too scientific to understand unless one happens to study Arabic, especially when the reading on the coin differs from the book and the illustrations are few and far between. There are not many English collectors who would care to learn Arabic in order to decipher these inscriptions, therefore for a book on this subject to be of much use every coin in it should be illustrated and an efficient description given. With these facts thrust, as it were, before me, the idea occurred to me, to

make a handy little text book for the use of myself and any numismatic friend who might be interested but, like myself, was unable to locate his coins when they bore their inscriptions in Arabic.'

The 'handy little text book', which he produced in his own calligraphy, was published in 1911 by direct photography. It was entitled *Modern Copper Coins of the Muhammadan States of Turkey, Persia, Egypt, Afghanistan, Morocco, Tripoli, Tunis etc*.

Even the title page was designed in his own careful handwriting and contained a drawing of the puzzling coin that had started him on his road to collecting. The book included maps of the relevant territories and was republished, as a joint British-American publication, in 1969. It was followed by three more on the same line of collecting, two in 1914 and one in 1921. These have not so far been republished.

The investor-collector goes about forming his collection in a different way. He looks around for a dealer who specializes in coins for investment. There are many, brought into being by the widening interest in coin collecting in all its

8 *Mahogany coin cabinet, with trays pierced to hold coins of different sizes. Trays are usually interchangeable within the cabinet.*

9 *At coin auctions, such as this one at Sotheby's, the prospective buyers remain seated while the coins are brought round and shown to each in turn.*

10 a

10 b

10 a, b *A collector's piece : the 'Una and the Lion pattern £5', designed in 1839 for the new coinage of Queen Victoria. It was never in general circulation, although many pieces were struck from the dies.*

11　*Students Room in the Department of Coins and Medals at the British Museum, London.*

phases; by the modern speculation in the possible rarities that may be found in money nominally in circulation; and by the proliferation of issues of limited numbers of single coins or sets of coins, either intended for circulation or simply as proofs of coins that are, will be or might be put into circulation. There is a lot here to explain: let us take it a step at a time.

In the last ten or fifteen years there has been a sudden awareness that there are, among modern coins—in Britain back to say 1816, when the coinage was reformed—rare pieces worth a premium. This has been known for a long time but only recently has it come to be general knowledge that such pieces appreciate in value if in reasonable condition and held by the collector over a number of years. The steady depreciation in the value of money

has forced on the appreciation of art forms in general. High prices realized at coin auctions by desirable pieces, and well reported in the press, have caused the investor to take a look at investment in coins, and the spiral has carried on from there. To meet the market many of the old established firms have set up separate departments simply to deal with modern coin investment.

So far as single coins are concerned, dealers and numismatic publishers have provided weekly, monthly, quarterly or annual lists showing approximate values for each of these modern coins, in several states of condition. Coin magazines and newspapers also publish such lists, while the long established dealers who have published monthly coin lists for many years include these modern

12   *For the Jubilee of Queen Victoria in 1887, the Royal Mint issued such sets of proof coins. At the time, however, these limited issues produced little purely investor interest.*

issues, as they always have. Thus the hunt was on. The investor and the man in the street started to look at the coins which passed through their hands, hoping to find a rarity, or at least a coin worth more than its face value to a dealer. Investors, studying the profusion of coin valuation lists, selected coins worth buying and sank capital in them, selling out when the market had risen—and it continued to rise steadily. All this speculation and investor interest brought in its wake the offering of coins in poor condition at premium prices and it is obvious that such coins should be shunned by the careful investor.

The merry-go-round of speculator coin buying, once started, trundled on at a steady speed. There was—is—little harm in it provided the riders obeyed the rules, the most important of which

is that any post-1816 modern coin which is badly worn, damaged, scratched or otherwise rendered in poor condition, is not a coin which will appreciate in value. I have been frequently criticized for my unyielding stand on the matter of coin condition, and I maintain that stand. After thirty-five years in coin dealing I have seen so many people bring me coins in poor condition, and even though they were rare I may have had to send them away disillusioned—frequently doubting my judgment. I can only repeat: the condition of any and every modern coin is of the first importance.

With the issues of limited numbers of single coins or sets of coins the market is safer, since the matter of coin condition does not arise. Such pieces are usually struck as proofs, a term which will be explained.

The issue of limited numbers of single coins, or sets of coins, goes back so far as Britain is concerned for around one hundred and fifty years. When Queen Victoria came to the throne in 1837 a new coinage was obviously needed. Among the various designs one, intended for a piece of the value of £5, was produced. To the student-collector it is known as the 'Una and the lion pattern £5'. In the event this attractive piece was not adopted for general circulation but a considerable number were struck from the dies and became collector's pieces. They are expensive, but a good investment—if you can get one. By 1887, with the issue of the Jubilee coinage of Queen Victoria, the matter of issuing limited numbers of sets of proof coins was being taken seriously by the Royal Mint. There had been such sets before, back as far as the reign of George IV (1820–30), but these had been assembled by persons in the higher ranks at the Mint, or by jewellers. The 1887 sets, however, were official Mint offerings. Though they were taken up by collectors and investors there seems to have been little purely investor interest in their purchase.

When the much criticized Jubilee coinage of Victoria was redesigned in 1893 further sets of proof coins were offered by the Royal Mint, as well as single coins, £5 and £2. These single coins had also been offered in 1887. Again the sets were taken up, but again there seems to have been little purely investor interest in these limited issues.

It should here be explained that a proof coin is a specially struck, highly polished and superbly finished example of a coin which goes into circulation. Naturally proof coins do not circulate but are collector's pieces, pure and simple. Non-proof £5 and £2, dated 1887 and 1893 respectively, were struck, but there is no evidence that they were actually put into circulation, at a time when gold Sovereigns and Half-sovereigns were daily in use. Non-proof sets of 1887 and 1893 coins were put together and sold in fitted cases, as were the proof sets, but the former were probably assembled by jewellers and coin dealers.

The precedent of offering proof sets when a new coinage design was introduced having now been

13 *Sets of proof coins were issued when the coinage was redesigned in 1937. This set, originally offered at 30s, is now worth around £60.*

14 *There is money to be made by investing in limited numbers of proof sets such as this—'the first gold coinage of the Isle of Man 1965. One of 1000 proof sets'.*

15 *Every possible care must be taken in cleaning and housing coins, however valuable they may be. Gold, silver, cupro-nickel, copper and bronze may all deteriorate or become damaged unless precautions are taken.*

16 *Coin dealers come to know their clients' requirements through personal contact. A collector is advised to buy through a dealer, rather than to 'go it alone' at auction sales and antique shops in the hope of a 'find'.*

13

14

established, proof sets of the new coinage were offered by the Royal Mint when Edward VII (1901–10) ascended the throne. They were followed in turn by proof sets in 1911 (George V), 1927 when the coinage was redesigned, 1937 (George VI new coinage), 1950 (half century), 1951 (Festival of Britain), and 1953 (Elizabeth II new coinage, with no gold pieces).

The 1937 sets of proof coins were offered in two categories. Set A consisted of the four traditional gold coins, £5, £2, £1 (Sovereign) and 10s (Half-sovereign), plus set B. Set B consisted of all the silver and bronze coins then in circulation— 5s, 2s 6d, 2s, 1s (English), 1s (Scottish), Sixpence, Threepence, and Maundy Money consisting of 4d, 3d, 2d and 1d; and in bronze 1d, ½d and ¼d, together with the then new twelve-sided 3d in nickel-brass. Some 20,900 such sets were sold. The A set was offered at £21, value now around £300. The B set was offered at about 30s, value now around £60.

It was small wonder that the world began to wake up to the investment value of the limited issue of proof sets. In fact both sides, the issuer and the investor, became aware of the money to be made. By the 1950s things were beginning to gather speed. Newly formed countries, older countries, independent island governments and the like saw a substantial revenue to be gained. The investor saw money to be made. The issue of limited numbers of proof sets, individual proof coins, and 'first year' issues of new coinage offered in plastic containers, has now become big business, and the investor-collector market has come into being. A by-product of the boom is that the prices of all coins, especially the modern coins we have been considering, have risen sharply, which makes collecting much more expensive for the student-collector, although from his point of view the position will probably right itself in time. When what are now current coins become collector's pieces the better-condition coins will interest the student-collector. They may rise a little more in value, or they may fall. Either way the market will probably level off, and the student-collector will be able to assess with reasonable certainty the cost of embarking on a collecting theme.

15

16

ORIGINS OF THE COIN

Before coins evolved trade had to be carried on by barter. The Ancient Egyptians are frequently taken as an example of a nation which succeeded in attaining a very highly developed civilization and maintaining it without having money as we know it in later times. They were fortunate in having access to what was probably the richest gold-producing country in the ancient world. There were two main areas, Upper Egypt and Nubia, the deposits being mainly between the Nile and the Red Sea, between the 26th and 23rd parallels of latitude.[1] The river systems in this area had scoured the gold-bearing rocks and it was, in the first instance, the alluvial gold which was collected by the now age-old system known as panning. Archaeological evidence indicates that gold objects appeared in Egypt at about the end of the fifth millennium BC and the start of the fourth.[2] Shallow surface mining was also undertaken in the Nubian area. Mining gold gradually developed and, according to surviving accounts, the mines were worked by slave labour.

Copper was also a metal in use from about 5000 BC. Cyprus had large deposits and there were, and still are, considerable quantities both there and in Africa. No specific date can, obviously, be given at which copper began to be alloyed to produce the harder metal, bronze. The Late Bronze Age in the Mediterranean area is given as about 1600 BC and in the Early and Middle Bronze Ages the various peoples surrounding that sea are thought not to have had a great deal of contact with each other. By about 1800 BC the Kassites had seized Babylonia, the great civilization of the Tigris-Euphrates area, and the Hyksos invaders from Syria had conquered Egypt.

By 1600 BC great economic changes were taking place in the ancient world. In Egypt the period is that of the beginning of the New Kingdom, in Crete and Hellas the Late Minoan I period and the Late Helladic period. Part of these changes were due to the horse, which had helped the Hyksos to conquer Egypt around 1800 BC. The Egyptians, now gradually adopting its use in turn, threw off the yoke of their conquerors and, abandoning their ancient isolation, advanced into Asia in a series of wars of revenge. The horse now began to have an economic significance. The Egyptians and, no doubt, other nations, having learned its use, began to protect trading caravans, whose personnel and goods were carried by the slower camel and donkey. 'Armed convoys', it might be said, began to venture further and the nations that had met in battle made treaties of peace or alliance and trade among them began to increase and spread.

It was at about this point that the difficulties of trading by barter began to become acute. The peoples of the south, who had gold, came progressively into contact with others, whose wealth was in flocks and herds, 'and among such backward peoples the natural and obvious unit of value was the ox or cow . . . While the northerners and highlanders reckoned in cattle the Egyptians and the peoples of Mesopotamia were using gold, silver, electrum (a natural amalgam of silver and gold) and bronze, which they had learnt to weigh in the balance for the purpose of estimating its value'.[1]

As the various peoples from around the shores of the Mediterranean and from further

---

[1] Sutherland, *Gold, its Beauty, Power and Allure*
[2] Ibid

[1] Seltman, *Greek Coins*

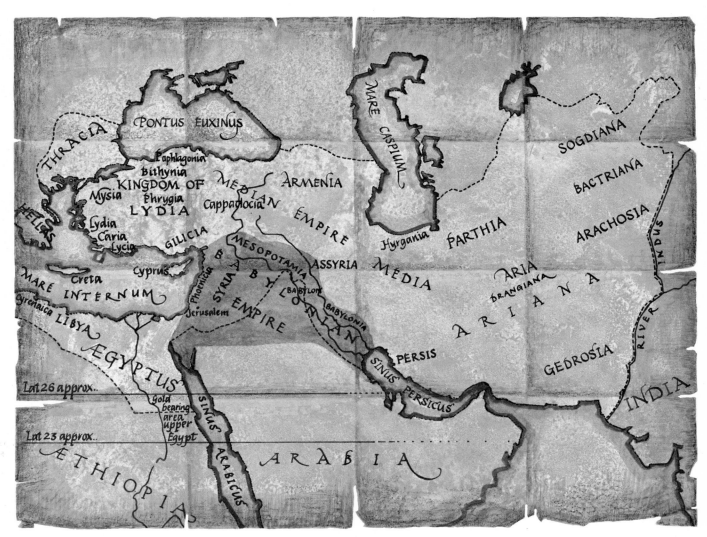

On map:

THRACIA
PONTUS EUXINUS
Paphlagonia
Bithynia
KINGDOM OF
Mysia
Phrygia
LYDIA
Lydia
Caria
Lycia
CILICIA
Cyprus
HELLAS
Creta
MARE INTERNUM
Cyrenaica LIBYA
Jerusalem
AEGYPTUS
Lat 26 approx.
gold bearing area upper Egypt
Lat 23 approx.
SINUS ARABICUS
AETHIOPIA
ARABIA

MEDIAN EMPIRE
ARMENIA
Cappadocia
MARE CASPIUM
Hyrcania
PARTHIA
MEDIA
MESOPOTAMIA
ASSYRIA
Phoenicia
SYRIA
BABYLON
BABYLONIA
BABYLONIAN EMPIRE
PERSIS
SINUS PERSICUS

SOGDIANA
BACTRIANA
ARACHOSIA
ARIA
DRANGIANA
ARIANA
INDUS RIVER
GEDROSIA
INDIA

afield began to meet in trade, the ox seems to have become a unit of value. This soon made things difficult. The Egyptians and Semites, with their linen and dyed wool, with rings and other articles of gold and electrum; the Hittites with their silver and cattle and the Cypriots with ingots of copper, tried to solve their various trading equations with such an object as an ox. It was obvious that, while you could divide the metals and manufactured goods, the ox must remain whole and alive, otherwise his value decreased!

Because of this indivisibility the ox became a standard to which the metals were adjusted. A gold equivalent could be a small pellet, a bar or a ring of a given weight, equivalent now to about 8·5 grammes. Copper was not so easy to deal with, the value of an ox being an ingot which weighed about 60 lbs. While the Greeks called these units a talanton, by their scale a copper or bronze talent weighed some three thousand times as much as the little piece of gold. The heavy copper and bronze talents began to be cast in the shape of an ox-hide,

17 *This map shows the greatest extents of the Babylonian (560 BC) and Persian (525 BC) Empires.*

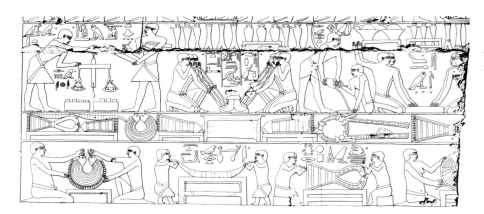

18 *This detail from a Sakkara tomb-relief (about 2500 BC) shows Egyptian goldsmiths at work. Note the scales, blowpipe and furnace.*

from which the head and tail had been removed. For various reasons, sometimes that of a metal shortage, these hide-shaped talents varied in weight. This reason is given for the difference in weight between a Cypriot piece, 37 kilogrammes, and an Achaean piece, 25½ kilogrammes, the metal being plentiful in Cyprus.

Other systems evolved, also based on weights. The Babylonians had a gold shekel, weight 8·34 grammes, and a base metal piece, a biltu, weighing 30 kilogrammes. These people, having a better mathematical ability, evolved a third weight unit, the manah, and related the three together:

1 shekel, weight 8·34 grammes
60 shekels = 1 manah, weight 500·40 grammes
60 manahs = 1 biltu, weight 30,024·00 grammes

Stone weights in the form of ducks have been found in Nineveh, some with interesting inscriptions, such as the name of the ruler, Dungi, circa 2472 BC and the value 'ten manahs'. Another with the inscription 'the palace of Eriba-Marduk King of Babylon, thirty manahs' shows that such weights were in use for a considerable time, this latter king having lived about 770 BC. Calculated by the weight of the stone ducks a manah of about

19 *The horse began to effect the economic situation in Egypt around 1600 BC, both in its use in the wars in Asia and in the protection of trading caravans. (Detail from a painted chest of Tutankhamen c. 1358-1349 BC, now in the Egyptian Museum, Cairo.)*

500 grammes evolved. This helped with the calculating problems and the Greeks and probably the Ionians had, between about 1000 and 800 BC, adjusted the weight of their own talent, adopting the manah under the name of mna. They had come across the manah through contact with the Phoenician traders.

Of course, the gramme had not yet been invented. The various pieces were equated by weight in the numbers shown, the resultant being translated into the later system to give us some idea in modern terms of the weights involved.

Though coins had still not been invented, vast accumulations of wealth were built up. The Egyptian kings and merchants, whose wealth was mainly in gold, needed some secure place in which to keep it. Where better than in a palace treasury or in a temple, whose sacred purpose would provide protection? These are the origins of banking. Valuables were stored in strongly-built, well guarded treasure-houses. Accurate records were kept, both of receipts and expenditure, with dates and the names of the depositors.

Such accounts were often kept on clay tablets. When the great palace of Cnossus in Crete was being excavated by Sir Arthur Evans such a tablet was found, recording the deposit of ox-hide copper talents in the royal treasure-house. The tablet was inscribed with the outline of a talent, two vertical columns each of three horizontal strokes, a balance, a vertical column of three strokes, another of two strokes, two vertical strokes, one above another; two marks like the letter S in reverse and two further vertical strokes. Sir Arthur read this inscription as an equation. Sixty ox-hide ingots (taking the six horizontal strokes as the sign-value of ten each) were weighed in the balance and found equal to $52\frac{1}{2}$ talents. The five horizontal lines and the other marks to the right of the balance giving the figures $52\frac{1}{2}$ meant that the talents were under weight, since they should have weighed a full sixty talents, each one being, as we have seen, the weight of one talent. The fact that they were under weight had, therefore, to be duly recorded.

As far as is known the treasuries of Egypt and Crete were used only to serve the royal household; that is, there were no facilities for merchants

and private traders either to deposit or borrow from the treasury. In Babylon, however, matters were taken a step further.

It is thought that the Babylonians independently evolved the treasure-house system and the keeping of accounts. The Semites soon saw further possibilities in the system and private persons were allowed to deposit valuables and gold for safe-keeping. A fee was charged for this service, which any rich merchant, liable to be travelling about, was glad to pay in return for the offer of security.

The next obvious step was soon taken. A merchant needing more capital received a loan in metal

20　*The ox becomes a unit of value. (Detail from a tomb in the Valley of the Kings.)*

Before the advent of the coin, Peloponnese currency consisted of rods or spits (obols) about 3 feet long. Six obols (a handful) were known as a drachma, a term eventually used as a unit weight of silver.

against securities in kind, a fee being charged by the 'banker' against the risk of the loss of the metal. Merchants were soon running regular accounts with the treasuries, which held securities of the merchants in exchange. Thus, in part, the system of banking and finance began to evolve even before coinage. The system is thought to have passed from Mesopotamia to Phoenicia and from there to the Greeks.

So the various methods of trading, the several systems of weights and measures, the various types of metals and other objects in use gradually came into being. No one system, particularly if it needed the equating of living objects with inanimate metal or manufactured goods, was necessarily easy to use within itself. When trade began to expand, in the way which has very briefly been outlined, the chaos of the market-place can well be imagined. Something which would be of recognized value on all sides was needed, and to fill this need the coin was evolved. Even so, its evolution was slow, nor has it now, after almost 2,700 years, evolved into one coinage system.

Coins are considered to have been evolved in the simplest way. We have seen various pieces of metal used in barter. The most convenient of these was the blob of gold or electrum, since its size and weight made it easily portable. What had now to be done was for a king or merchant, or a series of rulers or traders, to mark such 'dumps' in a manner which would be recognized among rulers and traders as its source of origin and its guarantee of value. Put more simply, if merchant A received from merchant B a blob of metal marked in a certain way, which both merchants recognized, merchant A knew that the mark had been put on the metal by merchant C, that it was his mark

of recognition and guaranteed that the metal was worth a stated amount. On this simple method grew up the whole system of exchange by money, the designing and minting of coins, their clipping and forgery, their increasing or lowering in intrinsic value and all the good and evil of the monetary system.

The marking of coin was evolved with no great difficulty. It is thought that an Ionian merchant hit upon the idea of impressing on a lump of gold a mark made with a sawn-off or broken nail. He knew the weight and value of the piece, and to save weighing it again when it once more passed through his hands, he put a recognizable mark upon it. Whoever thought of the idea, it came into being, and pieces

so marked went into circulation. Comparatively speaking there was not a large amount of 'money' in use in these ancient times, about 665 BC, so as soon as the marking had begun to take effect recognizable pieces came back through their marker's hands with reasonable frequency.

It is then suggested that the King of Lydia, seeing the merchant's marks, began to mark his gold 'coins' with his royal seal. Both methods of marking needed the use of a hammer to impress the mark, and in this simple way coinage came into being.

22 *Pre-coinage stone weights in the form of ducks.*

23 *The earliest forms of coin—gold Talent and Half-Talent from Cyprus (revs.).*

THE GREEKS

24   *Asiatic 'dumps' – electrum Staters from the seventh century. Note the nail-marks in cruciform shape.*

While the Hellenized Lydians had evolved coinage, it was left to the Greeks to make of it an art form. A word should first be said about them.

When the Greeks themselves spoke of Hellas they were usually referring to the peninsula of Greece. By the time of the evolution of the coin Greek civilization had spread to both sides of the Aegean Sea. It was to spread still further, to the borders of India and the shores of the Persian Gulf, through Egypt and the northern shores of Africa and through Italy and Sicily and parts of Spain. By the time of Alexander the Great (336 BC) the Greek Empire reached its greatest extent, as he drove his conquests further to the east.

Lydia was in what would now be called south-western Turkey and was one of the states which went to make up the Greek civilization. This empire as a whole was not a closely-knit body, but consisted of a number of separate city-states. It was not entirely unlike the British Commonwealth of Nations. The Greek city-states were entirely independent of each other, having different constitutions, laws, ways of life and means of defence, often with different ways of speaking the same language.[1]

The Greeks themselves always recognized Athens and Sparta as the most important of the city-states, but the many others must be taken into consideration if the Greek world as a whole is to be understood.

This collection of city-states warred amongst themselves. Numbers of combinations of city-states were formed, sometimes to fight each other and sometimes to meet a common enemy, but the failure of the states to unite as a whole sowed the seeds of their final destruction. In 431 BC the Peloponnesian War broke out and lasted for twenty-seven years. By the time Philip II of Macedon came to rule in 359 BC and began aiming at the domination of the Hellenic world, the city-states had begun to crumble. Sixteen years saw Athens itself crushed at last in 338 BC. In 336 BC Philip died. He was succeeded by his son, Alexander, who set about the subjugation of the east, pushing his conquests as far as India. The city-states were now too weak even to delay the main object of Alexander's campaign. At his death in 322 BC, and the suicide of Demosthenes, the Athenian opponent of both Philip and Alexander, the city-states fell apart for ever. The power of Rome was now in the ascendant and during the next centuries the Greek city-states came under its domination.

It was in this collection of city-states that coins began to take on an art form, to be skilfully designed and struck, many examples never having been surpassed for their beauty, and we therefore go back now to the nail and the seal of the King of Lydia. When the metal had been heated in a small furnace fired by charcoal, a blow with a hammer was needed to produce the impression. Many of the first coins produced were oval pieces of metal which were placed on a solid base of wood, stone or metal and had the nail-mark impressed on them. If the piece of metal were large enough more than one mark was made. Pieces exist where these marks take a cruciform shape, the central mark being elongated and flanked on either side by two lesser marks. Smaller pieces had a single mark, or possibly more than one mark, the two joining together.

It was probably soon noted that the reverse of the piece of metal picked up the impression of any irregularity of the surface on which it had been placed to be hammered. It appeared on the reverse, often in

[1] Freeman, *Greek City-States*

25 a

25 b

25 c

25 d

26 a

26 b

25 a, b, c, d, 26 a, b *Many Greek coins portray animals on their obverses—these silver pieces, from the sixth and seventh centuries, show a lion scalp, turtle, lion and bull, and a bull's head. The silver Stater from Corinth (26) shows Pegasus (obv.) and a swastika (rev.).*

28

27, 28 *Fine examples of Greek coin design: an ox-cart on an Octradrachm, and a lion and a bull on a Tetradrachm.*

27

29 *A detail from a mosaic showing Alexander at the Battle of Issus. His ambition was to see the fusion of Greek and Eastern cultures.*

30 a

30 b

30 a, b *A silver 4 Drachm piece from Athens : the goddess Athena on the obverse appears also on the reverse in the form of an owl.*

31 *Some of the best-known Greek city-states.*

the form of dot-like marks, or of lines that could possibly be the grain in a piece of hard wood. This no doubt led to the idea of marking both sides of a coin.

The seal impression eventually gave rise to the idea of striking coins with some artistic representation on them, from 'nails' on which a definite design had been cut, thus creating a primitive die. An electrum piece from the Thracian area, struck about the seventh century BC, shows a well executed rosette. Many of the known Lydian coins have a lion or a lion's head on one side and the 'nail-marks' on the other. These too are of about the seventh century BC, as are others of Ionia where a series of electrum pieces have a ram, an eagle, a horse or a head, said to be that of Heracles, on one side. Again the 'nail-marks' appear on the reverse. It is interesting to note that animals and birds found a place on coinage so long ago, a place which they have continued to occupy ever since. The head of Heracles points to the fact that eventually rulers' heads will begin to appear.

It was logical that each independent city-state should issue its own coinage. There are electrum

and silver pieces from Miletus, Ephesus, Phocaea, Chios, Samos, Aegina, Corinth and many others, struck in the seventh and sixth centuries BC. Athens itself appears to have issued coins at least as far back as 600 BC.

Dies were now beginning to be engraved with great skill, at least for one side of the coin. On a sixth-century BC silver piece of Samos is a lion scalp, while a small series of silver pieces of Aegina, struck in the seventh century, show a turtle. This was the 'coat of arms' of Aegina and probably started the custom, which soon developed, of having the city-state's 'badge' on its coinage. This little turtle 'is a clean, simple design, none the worse for being comical, for here is a nice, fat, porcine turtle'.[1]

At about the same time Corinth had on the obverse of its coins a fine winged horse, Pegasus, beautifully executed, while on the reverse is a swastika. Many people are not aware how far back this now maligned symbol goes—nor for how long man has had the ambition to fly, if not himself, then on the back of some form of animal with wings.

With artistic designs appearing

[1] Seltman, *Masterpieces of Greek Coinage*

34

33   *Greek gods were pictured as animals on items other than coins : a mirror case in relief shows Ganymede being carried away by Zeus (an eagle).*

32   *A map showing the extent of the Roman Empire in AD 300 and of the Byzantine Empire in AD 565.*

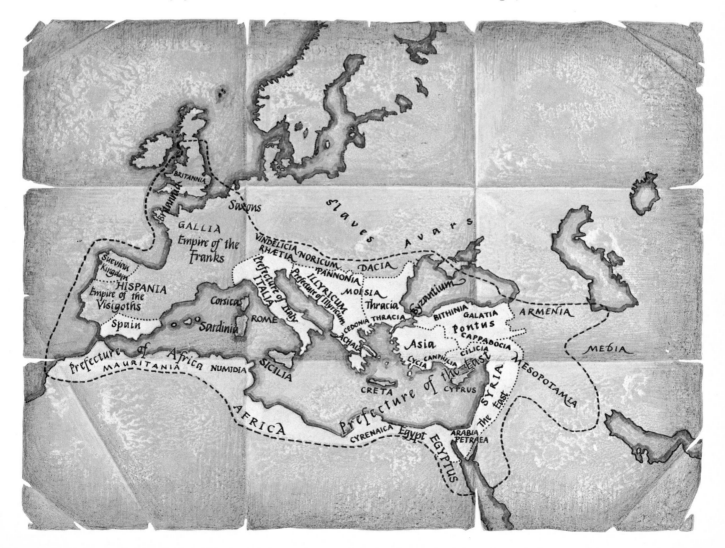

on coins, something of the method by which such designs were achieved is now of interest. It was previously pointed out that the whole theory of money at this time was based on a known weight of precious metal, marked in such a way that the device was the guarantee of the value of the metal by weight. The piece of metal to be marked would, therefore, first be weighed. It would be trimmed till it was of the required weight and would then be ready for striking.

A suitable solid object, such as a block of hard wood or a metal anvil—anvils can be of any shape to suit the work in hand and are not necessarily like those seen in a farrier's shop today—would form the base on which the striking would take place. Possibly the anvil would have an indentation cut into it to hold the lower die. It does not follow that at this time the indentation was of the exact shape of the die it was to contain: it would just prevent the die from jumping under the blow. Indentations of exact die-shape, later extended to confine also the flan of the coin and make it perfect in form, were to develop over the centuries. The lower die would, in

the early stages, probably be engraved on the anvil itself, but later a separate metal die would be made independently and placed in the indentation. The upper die would have its device engraved on the 'nail', which quickly became a punch, suitably shaped for its purpose.

The pre-weighed flan of metal would be placed on the lower die, having been heated in the charcoal furnace. The upper die would be placed on the flan of metal and struck with a hammer. The device on both dies, which were usually incuse—cut into the die—would now be imprinted in relief on the metal flan, and the finished coin was the result.

It would not be long before a stock of dies was built up, each differing in design for the various coins to be produced. It then became possible to combine different pairs of dies to produce different designs on coins. Mixing of dies in this way came to be known as muling. At the present time the term mule is usually used to describe a coin produced from two dies which ought not to have been used together. The use of the term

34

34 *A vase portrays Poseidon riding on a sea-horse.*

35 a, b *Silver 2 Drachm piece from Acragus—eagle (obv.) and crab (rev.).*

36 *River-bull on reverse of 4 Drachm piece from Gela.*

37 *Apollo on a silver Stater from Caulonia (obv.).*

38 a, b *Magnificent Dechadracm showing four dolphins (obligatory on coins from Syracuse) circling the head of Arethusa, the nymph of the fountain of Arethusa in the island of Ortygia near Syracuse. Chariots, too, were frequently found on Syracuse coins.*

35 a

35 b

36

37

has some elasticity, however, and can be used in the ancient context.

This simple method of producing coins, though it developed over the centuries, remained basically the same over a long period of time. It lasted, so far as Britain is concerned, until AD 1662 when primitive machines were at last accepted in the Royal Mint for rolling metal and striking coins.

The custom of putting the city-state's recognizable symbol or 'arms' on Greek coins continued to flourish. Athens is famous for its owls, which appear in various poses, sometimes with wings folded, sometimes spread. The goddess Athene was, like many other of the Greek gods and goddesses, credited with the power of assuming animal or bird shape. Zeus was supposed to appear as an eagle, Apollo as a falcon and Aphrodite as a dove. Athene usually appeared as an owl. Many coins of Athens show Athene on the obverse and an owl on the reverse. At the Battle of Marathon, fought at a time when Athens was establishing itself as the leader in art in Greece, soldiers saw the vision of an owl flying above them.

Apart from city-state symbols, we find gods and goddesses, events and legends, religion and politics, all taking their place on fine Greek coins as the art of coin-making developed. Syracuse has a long series of coins showing four-horse racing chariots. There are many varieties of this type. In some all four horses are plainly seen; in others they mask one another. On some pieces Agon, god of the Games, drives the chariot; in others his place is taken by Persephone. Nike, a winged victory, flies over the chariot, holding out a victor's crown. On the other side of many of these coins is the head of the goddess Artemis-Arethusa, with a number of dolphins circling round. Some of this series also carry the signature of the artist who cut the dies, a feature which in one form or another, usually initials only, is often found on modern coinage.

So the art of coin production grew and spread over the Ancient Greek world. Looking at some of these fine pieces now it is easy to see something of the attraction which they have for the collector and student. Many of them are looked upon as the finest coins struck in any age.

38 a

38 b

MACEDONIA

Thermaic
Gulf

THRACIAN SEA

AEGEAN SEA

Ambracian
Gulf

IONIAN SEA

Euboean
Gulf

MARATHON

Attica

Gulf
of Corinth

ATHENS

CORINTH

Aegina

SPARTA

Gulf
of
Argos

Gulf
of Messenia

Gulf
of
Laconia

MEDITERRANEAN SEA

CRETAN

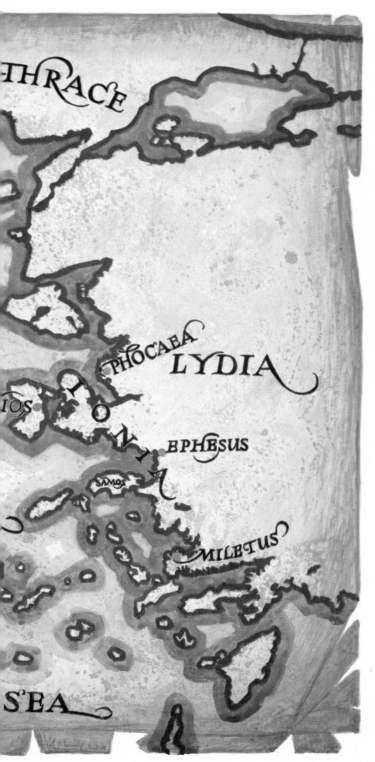

39   *Map of Ancient Greece.*

40   *Reverse of a silver Tetradrachm,*
c. 410 BC, Syracuse.

THE ROMANS

41 c

41 a

41 b

So far as is known bronze was used by the Romans as long ago as the third century BC in a form of coinage. Weights varied and the 'coins' changed hands on a weight basis. Starting as pieces of metal, probably irregular in shape, they later developed into bars or brick-shaped pieces of fixed weight, though these weights differed in various parts of Italy.

In Rome a local type of this form of coinage grew up. It consisted of large pieces of bronze called *aes grave*, 'heavy bronze', and these pieces were struck to a definite weight. The unit of reckoning was the pound, and this was divided into twelve ounces. A scale of values by weight evolved, as follows:

As = 1 pound (12 ounces) mark of value 1
Semis = $\frac{1}{2}$ pound, mark of value S, for Semis
Tremis = 4 ounces, mark of value . . . .
Quadrans = 3 ounces, mark of value . . .
Sextans = 2 ounces, mark of value . .
Uncia (ounce) = 1 ounce, mark of value .

This system of coinage on its own was found to be too clumsy and heavy to be acceptable by the Greek cities of Italy and the states of Central Italy, which had succumbed to Rome. A more facile type had to be evolved.

This took the form of a series of silver pieces of various types with the inscription ROMANO or ROMA, 'of the Romans', and although these pieces had a definite relationship with the original *aes grave*, the system was complicated by the successive changes in the weights of both types.

A new system adopted towards the end of the war with Hannibal comprised three denominations in

41 a, b, c *The head of Emperor Hadrian on an As of c. AD 126 is strikingly similar to the bronze bust (41c), which was recovered from the Thames.*

42 a

42 b

42 a, b *An elephant graces the obverse of a Pius Scipio Denarius (c. 46 BC).*

silver—the Denarius, the Quinarius and the Sestertius—with seven additional denominations in bronze, down to Semuncia or half ounce. The Denarius, still retained as the 'd' in our £sd, was at first equated to ten bronze Asses. These were struck coins of much less weight than the *aes grave,* which had been made by casting. Later the equivalent was altered to sixteen Asses. The Quinarius was rated at half a Denarius, and the Sestertius at a quarter of a Denarius.

A few gold pieces, extremely rare, were struck, the metal having been acquired by war and by tribute, but in the main the system given above served the Roman Republic from 213 BC down to about the last fifty years of that form of government.

A board of three officials, the *Tresviri auro argento aere flando et feriundo*—the 'three men concerned with the casting and striking of gold, silver and bronze'—was set up to control the Roman Republican issues. At first these officials are unknown to us by name, being considered of little importance in the Roman 'civil service' scale. Later the names of one and sometimes two of the three were placed on the coins which they issued. This fact gives an added interest to the collecting of Roman Republican coins, as well as being of importance to the Roman historian, since, like most Roman officials, the three held their office for only one year. By consulting surviving records it is possible to date such coins by putting the 'moneyers'' names in correct order.

This custom soon became official. The three may even have been compelled to sign their coins, since they were fully responsible for the quality of the metal and the correct weight of their coins. Their anonymous position gave the possibility of some corruption. This system of placing 'moneyers''

names on coins appeared in Britain on the Anglo-Saxon and Norman Pennies, for similar reasons.

During the last years of the Roman Republic and the struggle for the control of Rome, it became the custom for the various contestants to put their portraits on the coins which they caused to be struck for their respective armies. With this change began the period of the coinage of the Roman Empire.

The heads of important people appeared, such as Caesar, Brutus, Pompey and Mark Antony. Octavian, who later became the first Roman Emperor, taking the name of Augustus, not only put his head on the coinage, as did every Roman Emperor after him, but started a regular gold coinage, known as Aurei, and again reformed the coinage. The silver Denarius and the Quinarius were continued, but the Sestertius was struck in brass. The gold coins probably had only a limited circulation. They were changed for lower denominations by traders. The table of Roman denominations now looked as follows:

1 Aureus = 25 Denarii
1 Quinarius Aureus ($\frac{1}{2}$ Aureus) = 12$\frac{1}{2}$ Denarii
1 Denarius = 4 brass Sestertii
1 Quinarius (silver) = 2 brass Sestertii
1 Sestertius = 4 copper Asses = 2 brass Dupondii
1 Dupondius = 2 copper Asses
1 As = 4 copper Quadrantes ($\frac{1}{4}$ Asses)

This system was used for over two hundred years, Caracalla (AD 211-17) adding a coin known as the Antoninianus, called after himself, his official name being Antoninus. This new coin was a silver piece, larger than the Denarius and considered to be twice its value. It

43 a

43 b

43 c

43 a, b, c *The reverse of a Trajan Sestertius represents the State as the supplier of corn to the poor; (43 b, c) the Colosseum and the temple of Jupiter.*

44 a

44 b

45 a

45 b

eventually replaced the Denarius and was later struck in silver much alloyed with bronze. The Romans were no strangers to coinage debasement.

The Roman Imperial series is a most interesting one to collect. All the pieces, except the smallest of the copper denominations, have on the obverse the head of the Emperor, with his name and titles, among which were the number of times he had held the office of tribune of the people—shown as TRP—and consul—shown as COS, followed by Roman numerals.

The reverse types are very numerous. Almost all the then known gods and goddesses appear, as does such personification of qualities as VIRTVS MILITVM, 'the courage of the soldiers'. Public buildings, statues and arches, chariots and animals, the Emperor being greeted by notables from the provinces, the subjugation of Judea; these and many more form the subjects of a large and most interesting series of reverse types.

Thus we near the fall of the Roman Empire. The Goths, a German tribe, crossed the Danube frontier from the north in about AD 247, destroyed the province of Dacia and defeated and killed the Emperor Decius. Wave after wave of invasion followed till, in AD 410, Alaric the Goth sacked Rome itself. Later the Mongolian Huns entered the remains of the Empire, led by Attila who, though defeated at the Battle of Chalons in 451 by combined Goths and Romans, finally entered Italy in 452 and devastated it.

In the east the strong Persian Empire had come into being. Here, too, there was danger to the Roman frontiers. These were so far flung that armies could not be sent to defend any part attacked with sufficient speed to repel invasion, in spite of the famous Roman road system. The Empire therefore fell partly through lack of speedy transport. Seeing all these dangers in the late third century, the Emperor Diocletian appointed a colleague with a full share of imperial power to guard the west, while he continued the administration of the east. A generation later Emperor Constantine, the first to accept the Christian faith, moved the capital of the Empire to a city whose location on the Bosphorus between

44 a, b, 45 a, b   Sestertii of Trajan and Nero showing on their reverses a bridge over the Danube, and the harbour at Ostia.

46, 47, 48, 49   More Emperors— Brutus (46), Anthony (47), Trajan (48) and Caligula (49) (obvs.).

46

47

48

49

the Black Sea and the Mediterranean had impressed him as a good central point for the co-ordination of the defences of the eastern frontiers. This city was called Byzantium. The Emperor renamed it after himself, Constantinople. Thus came into being the Eastern Roman Empire, which held out against the invaders for more than a thousand years after the fall of Rome. It was finally destroyed by the taking of Constantinople by the Ottoman Turks in AD 1453.

The Eastern Roman Empire, magnificent in its richness, gave rise to a series known as the Byzantine coinage, in which gold coins are almost more common than those in lesser metals. They are of considerable collector interest and, with the rise of Christianity, show many religious subjects. A Christ-figure frequently appears, as do saints, crosses and, of course, the Emperor or Empress.

50 a

50 b

51

50 a, b   *A gold Numisma, a coin typical of the Byzantine period: on the obverse the bearded Emperor Jean II Comnenus (1118-43) stands beside the Holy Virgin Mary, while the reverse carries the figure of Christ.*

51   *St Michael (right) stands beside Emperor Isaac II Comnenus, on the obverse of a gold Numisma.*

52, 53   *Gold Solidus of Justinian II Rhinotmete and Constans II (obvs.).*

54   *Very similar to many Byzantine coins is this eleventh-century medallion of St Peter. Made of enamel on gold, it is one of a set on an ikon formerly in a monastery at Jumati, Georgia.*

55   *Rome falls to the Goths led by Alaric, AD 410.*

52

53

54

55

THE SPREAD OF COINS IN EUROPE

56 a

56 b

57 a

57 b

56 a, b *Gold Ducat from Venice, 1284.*

57 a, b *A Papal coin—silver Grossone of Gregory XI, 1371-8.*

The Roman Empire at its greatest extent was responsible for the spread of Roman coinage in all that part of Europe south of the Rhine and Danube rivers. The gradual contraction of the power of Rome still left, for a time, Roman coins in use. In Britain the withdrawal of the legions caused a shortage of coinage, especially in precious metals, which soon became hoarded.

On the mainland of Europe, following the fall of Italy in and after AD 452, a number of puppet emperors ruled for a time. Of these Romulus Augustus was the last, being deposed by Odovacer, the chief of the Heruli, in 476. He issued coinage based on the Roman style, but with his own portrait.

A further invasion of Italy took place in 489, this time by the Ostrogoths, that is, the eastern Goths. They assassinated Odovacer in 493 and assumed the mastery of Italy under Theodoric. Gold, silver and bronze coins continued to be issued, this time imitating those being struck by the Emperor of the Eastern Roman Empire in Constantinople. Theodoric ruled from 493 till 526 and certain of the gold pieces issued during this period went so far in imitation as to carry the portrait and titles of the Byzantine Emperor of that period, Anastasius. They are therefore difficult to separate from the true Byzantine coins.

Theodoric was followed by Athalaric (526–34) and he by Theodahad (534–6). These and the later Ostrogothic kings continued to issue coins, largely imitative of Roman or Byzantine pieces, or of each other, but frequently carrying the portrait of the ruler in question. The main conclusion is that at this period none of the rulers decided upon a drastic reform of the coinage, as we have seen twice previously during the Republican and Empire periods. There was probably neither the time, the need nor the inclination for this, as the period was one of continual strife. Any form of settled trade must have been brought almost to a standstill or at least carried on under the most difficult conditions.

It was not to be expected that the Romans would stand by and see their Empire decimated by the invaders. Justinian I (527–65) made great re-conquests of western provinces and from his reign till that of Basil I (867–86) the Byzantine emperors struck coins at mints in Italy, mainly at Rome and Ravenna. These are usually classified under the Byzantine series.

Continual struggles and shifts in power went on for many centuries. Charlemagne crossed the Alps in 774, forced the submission of the Lombards and issued coins from Roman mints. Papal coins began to appear during the time of Pope Adrian I (772–95). In 962 Otto I was crowned Emperor on his deposition of Berengarius II, King of Italy, and the then Holy Roman Empire passed to the Saxon kings of Germany, who passed it on to their successors. The period of coinage of the German emperors lasted from the tenth to the thirteenth century. From the thirteenth to the fifteenth century Italian history is that of the Later Middle Ages during which, though technically a single kingdom, Italy was in fact composed of a large number of independent states, not unlike the city-states of the Greeks. Many of these were ruled by powerful families and kingdoms, whose names are familiar even now, such as Milan, Naples, Sicily, Genoa and Venice. These and others usually issued their own coinage, which gradually began to take styles different from that of Rome. Venetian Ducats are familiar by name to us all, if only through *The Merchant of Venice.*

58 a

58 b

60 a

60 b

59 a

59 b

61 a

61 b

58 a, b   *From the reign of Edward III, an Anglo Gallic gold Ecu, 1337.*

59 a, b, 60 a, b   *France: A silver Testoon minted in the reign of Francis I, and a Henry III silver Franc (60 a, b).*

61 a, b   *An example of the famous Spanish 'Pieces of Eight' – a silver 8 Reale piece (Philip II).*

The next phase covered the period from the Italian Renaissance to the revolution and the Napoleonic wars, from the mid-fifteenth to the late eighteenth century. The trend during this long period was one of consolidation, the smaller city-states tending to disappear.

A little thought over this very brief sketch of events in Italy will lead to the conclusion that the coinage story is one of the greatest complexity. Briefly, anyone with ruling power was likely to issue coinage. Some were based on Roman issues, some on Byzantine. Others copied north African – Arabic – coinages and the power of such states as Venice produced great issues of coins which became world known.

The spread of coinage through France is equally complex. Robert Carson[1] clarifies the situation by dividing the development into six successsive stages. These are: (1) 'the imitative coinage of the barbarian kingdoms which replaced the Roman province of Gaul'. This covers the period of the Visigoths, Burgundians and Merovingians, from the fifth century till 751. (2) 'the new silver Denier coinage of the Carolingian kings and emperors', 751–987, (3) 'the Denier coinage of the feudal lords and the Capetian kings from Hugh Capet to Louis VIII', 987–1126, (4) 'the coinage from Louis IX to Charles VIII, marked by the introduction of the larger silver Gros and the re-emergence of gold', (5) 'the coinage of the Bourbons up to the Revolution', 1498–1792, and (6) covers the decimal coinage till the Fifth Republic, 1792–1960.

Here again there is the gradual emergence of a coinage, at first copying Roman and Byzantine types and then diverging into many, gradually to be consolidated as France began to take something of its present shape. The student has, again, a great field to cover, though after Hugh Capet catalogues exist which trace the gradual emergence of a French coinage, as opposed to regal and feudal issues which, at the beginning of the period, were being issued side by side. Modern French coinage can, perhaps, be regarded as having commenced with the reign of Louis XII in 1498.

[1] R. A. G. Carson, *Coins, ancient, mediaeval and modern*

62 'Pieces of Eight' . . . buried treasure . . . sunken galleons . . . dreams of unimaginable wealth have haunted men for centuries . . . .

63 b

63 a, b *Maria Theresa Thaler, with the date 1780. They are in fact still being minted.*

64 a, b *A gold 8 Escudos piece, with the head of Philip V and dated 1743. This was minted in Mexico when it was under Spanish rule.*

64 a

64 b

65 a

68 a

65 b

66

68 b

67

65 a, b *A fine example of a Thaler is this silver piece from Augsburg, produced in Emperor Ferdinand III's reign.*

66, 67 *Obverses of a Berthold II silver Bracteate, from Fulda in Germany (66), and a thirteenth-century silver Bracteate from Basel.*

68 a, b *Lively design on an Austrian silver Gulden, 1486.*

The new system established a gold coinage of denominations of twenty, ten, four and two Ducats and in silver of eight, four and two Reales. Variations were, of course, made to these denominations, but as a base they remained till 1808 when Spain was absorbed into the French Empire. Modern Spain can be said to have emerged from the Constitution of Cadiz in 1812.

Interest is added to the Spanish kingdom issues by the coins of the Spanish American mints, which were gradually established following the discovery of America. From this region, in coin or in bullion, came vast quantities of gold and silver, the 'Pieces of Eight' and the Spanish treasures which have engaged the attention of fiction writers and treasure hunters till the present day. At the creation of the kingdom of Spain in 1479 Portugal remained independent, having been created a kingdom by Alfonso I in 1112. Though held by Spain from 1580 till 1640 special Portuguese coinage continued to be struck.

The coinage of Germany is of great complexity, mainly because of the very great number of coin-issuing authorities. Even as late as the period 1700–1800 Davenport, in cataloguing only the Taler–Crown size coins—lists some ninety-five issuing authorities, some with smaller authorities within them. Carson, *op. cit.,* breaks down the whole series under eight headings and in a work of this kind no more can be done than list them, with a few comments. The divisions are: (1) 'coinages of the Merovingian and the Carolingian kings in so far as they affect Germany'. This covers the period from the sixth to the ninth century. The coinage of the Frankish kings was initially in imitation of Roman imperial gold pieces, but with the establishment of the new Carolingian dynasty by Pepin the Short (752–68) a new silver coinage of Denars, very like Britain's early silver Pennies, was established. This Denar or Denier of Pepin is held by some to be the origin of the English silver Penny and to have been copied by Offa. Oman[1] points out that Pepin's substitution of silver for gold in coinage was probably due to the fact that gold was, at this period, becoming rare all over the Western

The pattern in Spain followed, at first, much of the development seen elsewhere. Imitations of Roman coins were followed by 'local' issues in the small king-doms and districts, such as Navarre and Aragon, which emerged.

A single kingdom of Spain did not appear till the marriage of Ferdinand II of Aragon and Isabella of Castile in 1479. Though a coinage was still issued in several of the once separate kingdoms, modern Spanish coinage can be said to have originated from this period, when an ordinance of 1497 introduced a new monetary system.

[1] Charles Oman, *The Coinage of England*

world. The old Roman hoards had been exhausted and no supplies were coming from new mines.

Carson's next division is (2) 'the Denar coinage of the Saxon kings of Germany up to 1137'. In the light of what has just been said about the Denar the main type of coin is self-explanatory.

The next division is (3) 'the Bracteate coinage of Saxony and parts of Franconia and Swabia to the early decades of the fourteenth century'. The Bracteate was a peculiar type of coin. It was extremely thin, as though a Denar or Penny had been hammered even thinner, sometimes to almost twice its original size. The pieces were very fragile and could easily be broken. Indeed, they were so thin that they carried a device on one side only, in relief, while the reverse had the same design incuse. It is difficult to understand why such coins ever came into practical use and lasted for some two hundred years, or why the issues were so numerous. How numerous they were can be gleaned from the fact that Brandenburg, Pomerania, Prussia, Thuringia, Lower Saxony, Franconia and Swabia all issued this type of coin. In part this perhaps represented an attempt to continue a coinage in precious metal rather than issue a base metal coinage, though even base metals made their appearance in Europe during this period. Even so it would be thought that they could have been struck from the same amount of metal, at twice the thickness and half the diameter.

The next division, (4), covers 'the Denar coinage of the Hohenstaufen period, roughly also to the early fourteenth century in parts of Franconia and Swabia and the West'. The period of time is the same as (3), about 1150–1350, and in certain areas Bracteates and Denars were in circulation.

Section (5) covers 'the Groschen and late mediaeval gold, the period being from about 1300 to 1500'. The economy of western Europe was now recovering from the upheavals sparked off by the fall of Rome. Trade was increasing and gold once more began to come into general use for coinage. Issues throughout the German states were still very numerous, but were influenced by the French Gros Tournois, instituted by Louis IX

in 1266. This piece became accepted in trade fairly widely and was also copied. In Germany it became known as Groschen and was in common use from 1300. Local issues soon followed. In 1252 gold coinage in western Europe made a reappearance in the form of the Florin, struck in Florence, from which it takes its name. This piece, too, was accepted in Germany, and local gold issues soon followed. Issues as a whole were still complicated by a host of major and minor issuing authorities.

The situation begins to clear a little with section (6), 'the coinages of the more important modern states from 1500 to the Napoleonic period'. This covers the years from about 1500 till 1806. The issues and the numbers of different denominations are still very numerous. Gold was now in steady circulation and the Taler (or Thaler, Daler, Dollar), a large silver Crown size piece mentioned earlier, made its appearance. A similar piece, a Crown, value 5s, also appeared in England in 1551. There are many collectors who specialize in these fine pieces. Some idea of their number can be gleaned from the ninety-five and more issuing authorities mentioned above.

Section (7) covers the 'State coinage of Germany up to 1871' and (8) 'the coinage of united Germany'.

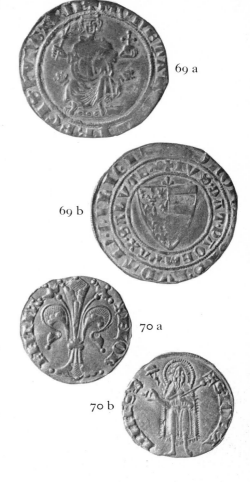

69 a, b, 70 a, b   *Silver Groschen from Hungary, and a gold Florin from the town that gave it its name—Florence.*

71 a, b, 72   *Czechoslovakia—a silver Joachimsthaler of Louis I, and the obverse of a silver Bracteate.*

THE COIN REACHES BRITAIN

73 a, b *An imitation of the head of Apollo appears on the obverse of this gold Gallo-Belgic Stater, c. 125-100 BC. By this time the chariot design on the reverse was becoming less well-defined.*

73 a

73 b

74 a, b *Gold Westerham type Stater. Here the design is almost unrecognizable.*

74 a

74 b

Coins reached Britain from the mainland of Europe. Waves of invaders from Belgic Gaul, probably coinciding with the Germanic invasion across the Rhine, brought with them coins known as Staters and Quarter-staters. These gold pieces were run-down designs which had been copied and recopied from the gold Staters of Philip II of Macedon, who acceded to the throne in 359 BC. The date of the first coins of this type is uncertain, but they have been placed at *circa* 125–100 BC. In the recopying over two centuries the original fine design, the head of Philip as Apollo on the obverse and a biga, a four-horse chariot with charioteer driving, on the reverse had become almost unrecognizable. The name of Philip appeared at the bottom of the original coins (technically—in the exergue). This has now disappeared as well. It has already been seen that this racing-chariot type reverse design was one that was popular with both the Greeks and the Romans. By the time copies of Philip's Stater reached Britain, at about the dates given above, the face on the obverse was still recognizable but the chariot had vanished and only a rough representation of a horse remained, surrounded with other symbols which could be the remains of the charioteer and a wheel.

On the smaller Quarter-staters the face disappears altogether on most examples, leaving only what had been part of the hair and the wreath which bound it. The horse on the reverse is just about recognizable. To judge by the places in which the majority of the pieces have been found, the invaders who brought them landed on the east and south-east coasts of Britain and settled in the eastern counties between the Wash and Beachy Head. As is often the case with finds of a particular type of coin, examples

have come to light outside this area, but they are few and isolated.

Another early coinage, tentatively dated 50 BC–AD 50, is the so-called tin money. This was not made by the invading Belgae, so far as is known, but the type seems to have come from central Gaul even so. The core of these pieces was copper, over which tin was washed, giving a silvery appearance when new, but rapidly deteriorating. This combination of metals has been called speculum on account of its shiny appearance.

The design is crude in the extreme. On the obverse appears a device not unlike a helmet. This is all that is left of the head of Apollo. The reverse contains a design which at first glance looks very like a trestle table seen side-on. This is all that remains of a charging bull. The coins were made by casting in strips and broken off as needed. Lugs still remaining on many of the coins show the point of junction.

A third wave of invaders arrived somewhere about the beginning of the first century BC and a fourth arrived after Julius Caesar had conquered Gaul. Caesar himself records that chieftains who had unsuccessfully resisted him took refuge in Britain. In part they are the reason why he undertook his two military expeditions into Britain—to prevent the Britons from sending reinforcements to the Gauls.

The coins brought by the third and fourth waves were again gold Staters. They were much like those we have already seen, uninscribed with any name and with only the remains of a head on the obverse and a rough horse, in some cases completely disjointed, on the reverse. Quarter-staters also arrived with these invasions. Hoards are again found all over the south-east of England, but reaching now as far north as the river Humber.

The coins brought in this way into

75 *The fine designs on these three Anglo-Saxon coins are still remarkably clear, despite having been buried for hundreds of years.*

76 *Some of the 101 Anglo-Saxon coins discovered at Crondall. Analysis of the hoard shows that a definite coinage was beginning to emerge in about AD 670.*

77 a

77 b

78

79

80

77 a, b   *A gold Stater of Tasciovanus, ruler of the Catuvellauni tribe (c. 20 BC–AD 10).*

78   *Tincommius gold Stater (obv.).*

79   *Verica gold Stater (rev.).*

80   *Iceni uninscribed gold Stater (rev.).*

Britain gave rise to a local issue of gold Staters, the first British gold coinage. So far as can be dated they were probably in use about 90–70 BC. For purposes of classification many of them are named after the spot at which the first of the types were found, such as the Westerham type, the Chute (Wiltshire) type, the Clacton type, and so forth. This has enabled numismatists to divide up the pieces from finds under these names, irrespective of where later examples of any one type were found.

In August 55 BC Caesar set sail for Britain with a fleet of about eighty ships, and this initial expedition having given him some idea of the opposition which faced him, his second was made in much greater strength. It says something for the power of Rome that on the northern shore of the Empire he could, between August 55 BC and the spring of 54 BC, assemble some eight hundred ships and the forces to man them. With these Caesar made his second landing but the Britons, seeing the size of the oncoming force, had taken to the hills. Caesar followed and a battle was fought at a spot which is not now known. After one final attempt in Kent to oust the Romans the fighting ceased and Caesar returned to Gaul in September, having demanded hostages and appointed a yearly tribute to be paid to Rome.

The large hoard of gold coins found at Whaddon Chase, Buckinghamshire, originally about two thousand in number, could have been the annual tribute money payable to Rome and it may have been stolen on the way and buried.

A final wave of refugees arrived in Britain after Caesar's campaigns in Gaul in 52 BC. It is thought unlikely that they brought any quantity of gold coins with them as gold coinage had been suppressed in Gaul.

A glance at the map will show the approximate areas occupied by the various tribes, as well as their names. They were left in peace by the Romans till AD 43, when the conquest of Britain was achieved by Claudius. These tribes continued to issue a gold coinage, designated Staters, with halves and quarters. In many cases the artistic style revived and some had the name or part of the name of the ruler on them. Tasciovanus (c. 20 BC–AD 10),

ruler of the Catuvellauni, has various abbreviations of his name– anything from TASC to TASCIAV –on his coins, while others are inscribed TASCIO RICON. Cunobelin (c. AD 10–40) has the name of the town of minting on some of his coins. This was Camulodunum, variously abbreviated, the site of the modern town of Colchester.

The position has now been reached when the various rulers of the tribes shown on the map usually issued coinage in gold, silver and bronze. With the exception of the coins of Durotriges, which are frequently covered with a meaningless number of dots and lines–the very lowest form to which the head and the horse descended– the artistic merit of the pieces is considerable, bearing in mind the limitations of the period. Some pieces still contain only part of a head, but some very good heads appear, as on some of the coins of Eppillus (AD 5–10), ruler of the Atrebates and Regni, and in particular on numerous pieces of Cunobelin. As several Roman historians mention this ruler, it is possible that he was in fairly close touch with the Romans. His coins certainly show some Roman influence.

Memories of the chariot linger on in many reverse types, a horse in various forms and sometimes a wheel appearing. There are some quite spirited horseback riders on several reverses, while various human beings appear on others.

To date, some seventy-eight hoards of Ancient British coins have been found, some quite small and others containing several hundred pieces. They come from as far apart as Jersey and Peeblesshire but the find-sites are mainly in the Midlands and the east and south of Britain, extending as far west as Devon and Gloucestershire.

Following the conquest of Britain by the Romans under Claudius in AD 43 the Roman monetary system was introduced and Roman coins began to circulate. There then followed a period of something over four hundred years in which the currency of the Roman Empire was the only coinage in use. Seaby[1] for purposes of simplification divides the coinage of the Roman occupation

[1] *Standard Catalogue of British Coins*

81   *The conquest of Britain by the Romans in AD 43 led to changes in virtually every aspect of the island's way of life : Britain uses Latin inscriptions on its coins even today.*

82   *In the pre-coinage era, barter was the accepted form of commercial exchange. Ancient Britons are here seen trading with Phoenicians.*

83   *Offa, King of Mercia, appears on the reverse of this silver piece, a Penny struck at Canterbury.*

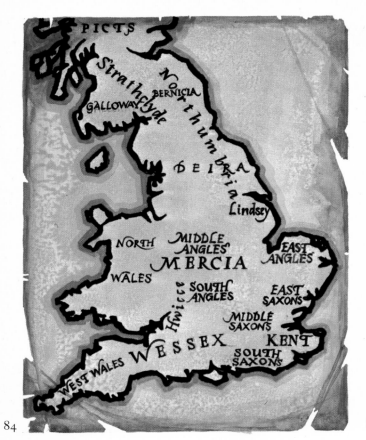

84, 85, 86 *Three phases of Britain's history. (84) is a map of Anglo-Saxon Britain, (85) shows the earlier distribution of the Ancient British tribes, and (86) is a later, self-explanatory map of the Mint Towns.*

into four sections. These are:

1. Roman emperors and usurpers whose coins were current in Britain or who counted 'Britannia' as one of their possessions.
2. Some coins that are particularly related to Britain by type or inscription.
3. Some of the coins struck in Britain, at London, Colchester, or elsewhere.
4. British imitations of Roman coins.

The first section is the largest and probably the most interesting. Its coins range from those of Julius Caesar, who was assassinated in the Senate in AD 44, to Honorius (393–423). Such famous names as Tiberius (AD 14–37), Caligula (37–41), Nero (54–68), Hadrian (117–38) and many others occur during this period. The coins are silver and bronze, the Denarius being probably the most common, though a certain amount of gold was struck during this period.

As with all Roman coins of this period, those with portraits are extremely interesting. That of Julius Caesar is particularly fine, telling something of the ability of the man who was, in fact, a very clever leader and administrator. It contrasts with the bull-necked

Vespasian (69–79) on his bronze As. The Denarius of Tiberius, showing his sharp-nosed face on the obverse and Livia seated on the reverse, was in circulation in the time of Jesus and is held by some to be the Tribute Penny of the Bible.

The coins under section (2) are of more direct interest to the collector of British coins, since they all mention Britain in one way or another. It must be remembered that Seaby's divisions overlap so far as the rulers are concerned. Thus we get Claudius once more, on a most interesting gold Aureus. His head occupies the obverse, and the reverse shows a typical Roman triumphal arch, inscribed DE BRITANN. There is a similar Denarius in silver, and both are rare pieces. As the actual conqueror of Britain, Claudius was 'awarded' this mark of triumph.

Section (3) starts with Carausius, the usurper in Britain and Gaul (287–93), some of whose pieces are very rare. The majority of the pieces in this section were struck either at London or Colchester.

The final small section of British imitations of Roman coins is of academic interest but the workmanship is not up to the Roman standard.

The withdrawal of the Roman

MINT TOWNS IN THE BRITISH ISLES

1 Berwick
2 Newcastle
3 Durham
4 Kingston-on-Hull
5 Hedon
6 Torksey
7 Rhuddlan
8 Lincoln
9 Derby
10 Nottingham
11 Castle Rising
12 Stafford
13 Lynn
14 Lichfield
15 Norwich
16 Leicester
17 Stamford
18 Tamworth
19 Peterborough
20 Coventry
21 Thetford
22 Huntingdon
23 Malmesbury
24 Cardiff

25 Southwark
26 Reading
27 Marlborough
28 Rochester
29 Soho and Birmingham
30 Warwick
31 Northampton
32 Bury St Edmunds
33 Cambridge
34 Ipswich
35 Hereford
36 Buckingham
37 Bedford
38 Pershore
39 Newport Pagnell
40 Sudbury
41 St Davids
42 Winchcombe
43 Gloucester
44 Pembroke
45 Cirencester
46 Aylesbury
47 Maldon
48 Hertford
49 'Gothanbyrig'— (site of)
50 Horndon
51 Wallingford
52 Cricklade
53 Durham House
54 Lewes
55 Southampton and 'Hamwic'
56 Shaftesbury
57 Hastings
58 Bramber
59 Pevensey
60 Petherton
61 Chichester
62 Bath
63 Bedwyn

64 Sandwich
65 Canterbury
66 Warminster
67 Dover
68 Guildford
69 Axbridge
70 Watchet
71 Hythe
72 Lymne
73 Wilton
74 Salisbury
75 Bruton
76 Romney
77 Langport
78 Winchester
79 Rye
80 Milborne Port
81 Ilchester
82 Cadbury
83 Taunton
84 Steyning
85 Crewkerne
86 Dorchester
87 Bridport
88 Twynham and Christchurch
89 Wareham
90 Lydford
91 Launceston
92 Totnes
93 Berkeley
94 Bamborough
95 Kelso
96 Roxburgh
97 Jedburgh
98 Dumfries
99 Crossraguel Abbey
100 Lanark
101 Renfrew
102 Glasgow
103 Dunbarton
104 Linlithgow
105 Dunbar
106 Edinburgh
107 Kinghorn
108 Stirling
109 St Andrews
110 Perth
111 Dundee
112 Forfar
113 Montrose
114 Aberdeen
115 Forres
116 Inverness
117 Corbridge

Carlisle (siege)

Scarborough (siege)

York

Pontefract (Siege)

Chester (also siege)

Newark (siege)

Shrewsbury

Aberystwyth

Hartlebury Castle & Worcester

Oxford

Colchester (siege)

Combe Martin (not proven)

Bristol

London (lost to the King in 1642)

Lundy (not proven)

Barnstaple

Bideford (not proven)

Appledore (not proven)

Exeter

Weymouth

Truro

Sandsfoot Castle

● indicates MINTS of CHARLES I 1629-1649

87 *Officers receiving and weighing coin at the Exchequer, about AD 1130.*

88 a, b *A gold Noble of Edward III (first issue). The intricate design shows the King standing in a ship, possibly a reference to the Battle of Sluys, 1340.*

89 *The gold Angel (here of Richard III's reign—obv.), and the Half-angel, were the only gold coins struck from the restoration of Henry VI to the introduction of the Sovereign in 1485.*

88 a

88 b

89

legions and the end of the supplies of Roman coinage left something of a numismatic vacuum. There are two schools of thought about the possibilities of coinage during the Dark Ages. One favours the theory that a series of clipped copper pieces and barbarous copies was struck during the period; the other that no recognizable coins circulated after the middle of the fifth century. Some light was thrown on the matter by the finding of the St Martin's Treasure at Canterbury, which must have been buried about the end of the sixth century, and by the Merovingian coins, called Tremisses and dated about 650, forty of which were found in the Sutton Hoo ship burial. Dr J. P. C. Kent[1] points out that the complete absence of Anglo-Saxon coins in this find is proof that none then existed. More light was thrown on the subject by the analysis of the contents of a hoard of 101 gold coins found at Crondall. Numismatic scholars do not entirely agree as to the exact date when the hoard was deposited but *circa* 670 is favoured by a number of them. Dr C. H. V. Sutherland[2] analysed the contents of the hoard, from which most of our knowledge of the Anglo-Saxon gold coinage is obtained. Dr Sutherland traced the development of this gold coinage as follows:

550–75 Intensified absorption of Merovingian coins in southern and eastern England.
575–600 First production in England of coins based on Merovingian models and often executed by Merovingian craftsmen. (These,

together with the 'romanizing' class, continued to be struck at intervals until *c.* 675.)
610–30 ? Operation of the Mint of London.
610–50 ? Operation of a mint or mints in Kent.
660–65 ? Possible institution of a mint in York.
675 Emergence of the silver (Sceatta) coinage.

All the dates are tentative and not all scholars agree with them.

To remove one possible terminological doubt: Merovingian is a term applied to the Frankish dynasty reigning in Gaul and Germany, founded by Clovis in AD 486. Dr Kent, *op. cit.*, points out that 'the marriage of the Merovingian princess Bertha with Æthelbert of Kent *c.* 580 marks the re-emergence of England into a place in European affairs'.

Whatever differences of opinion there may be over the dating of the Crondall Hoard coins, which were principally struck in south-east England, a coinage was beginning to emerge. According to Brooke[1] the earliest coinage that can definitely be regarded as Anglo-Saxon is in gold and was copied from the Merovingian coin called the Tremissis. This itself was a copy of the coin first introduced by Constantine the Great (d. 337) Emperor of Rome and founder of the Eastern Roman Empire, Byzantium and Constantinople; it remained in use in the Western and Eastern Empires till after the middle of the eighth century. In Anglo-Saxon documents it is mentioned occasionally under the name of Thrymsa, and its use was not of long duration. A silver coinage took

[1] J. P. C. Kent, *From Roman Britain to Saxon England* 1961
[2] C. H. V. Sutherland, *Anglo-Saxon Gold Coinage in the light of the Crondall Hoard*

[1] G. C. Brooke, *English Coins*

its place, the pieces being known as Sceattas. This Sceat coinage, followed by a series at first struck in base silver and then in copper, and called 'Stycas' by numismatists for the purpose of identification, remained in use in various parts and kingdoms of England till a coin known as a Penny finally emerged. Naming this (topically today) Brooke[1] calls it the New Penny and states that it 'is commonly said to have been introduced by the famous Offa, King of Mercia from 757 to 796', the Penny appearing 'during the last quarter of the eighth century'. Since this was written in 1932 other information has come to light and Mr Christopher Blunt has in his collection a unique Penny of Heabert, King of Kent about 764, which was probably struck at Canterbury. It has the King's name HEABERT with the word REX in monogram.

As will be seen from the map, Anglo-Saxon England was divided into various kingdoms. From the point of view of coinage issues the country from about 775 can be divided up into Northumbria, Kent, Mercia, East Anglia and Wessex. Between 737 and 924 these various kingdoms were ruled over by a total of about thirty-six kings. After 764, Pennies were issued by most of these kings, while during the same period four Archbishops of York and six Archbishops of Canterbury had the privilege of issuing Pennies from their own ecclesiastical mints.

Numismatically the picture is further complicated by the Viking Invaders. They established a Danish kingdom of East Anglia and a Scandinavian kingdom of York. The Pennies which the rulers of these kingdoms issued were similar to those which they found in use. In the payment of Danegeld English Pennies found their way to Scandinavia. It is not unexpected, therefore, that a vast number of important Anglo-Saxon coins are to be found in the Stockholm and Copenhagen museums. The outcome of the many Scandinavian invasions was the final triumph of Cnut (or Canute) who, after a long struggle and the dividing of England into two kingdoms, finally succeeded to the whole with the death of Æthelred II (popularly called the Unready) and the death of his son

Edmund, who was proclaimed King in London and held Wessex – the 'southern kingdom' – till his death. Cnut was proclaimed King of all England in 1016.

As it developed the Penny became a most interesting and important coin. For some two hundred years before Cnut, the name of the moneyer, that is, the person responsible for the striking of each individual coin, had appeared on it. As far back as the Styca coinage of Eanred, King of Northumbria (810–41), moneyers' names had appeared, in part as a form of guarantee that the coin was genuine and of correct composition and weight. At about the time of Æthelstan (924–39) the name of the mint town in which the pieces were struck also began to appear. These were often abbreviated, as LOND or LUND CIVIT for London, EXE for Exeter or WINCI for Winchester. This combination of moneyer's name and place of minting is of the greatest importance to the numismatist and historian as well as of interest to the collector.

One or two points of interest have to be taken into account at this point. The government of England at this time and for many years to come was not carried on from London alone. In order to govern, the King moved about and set up his court in various suitable towns. The administration and the law moved with him. Thus the whole machinery of government might be set up at Winchester, Canterbury, Hereford or York, to mention but a few suitable towns. The striking of coins would also take place in these cities, so that Pennies were struck there with the name of the town on them.

Because of the difficulties of travelling, the various towns of importance tended to be fairly self-centred and where it was expedient mints were set up in them. These are shown on the map under A for Anglo-Saxon, till 1066, but it does not follow that all these mints were in operation at any one time, nor does the map give any clue as to how long a mint worked in any one reign or in any one year. A little later, after the Norman Conquest, the question is posed as to whether dies were cut locally or sent out from London, either as required or as master dies to be copied locally. Over the centuries

[1] G. C. Brooke, *English Coins*

90, 91   *Two varieties of William I's Pennies, the 'bonnet' type (90) and the 'two stars' type (91) (obvs.). The Penny coinage was now firmly established and was to continue the sole denomination till Edward I's accession.*

90

91

there is evidence to support all these possibilities.

During the period 973–1066 eighty-seven mints were working in England. Their names are stated on the coins which they produced, as are those of the moneyer. These latter no doubt travelled about either with the movement of the administration, with the delivery of dies or for many other reasons.

The design and the development of the Penny during the long period of five hundred years while it was the sole coinage of England is fascinating study. A thin flan of silver varying at different periods from about the size of a modern Sixpence to that of a Shilling, but usually just between the two sizes— the diversity of its artistic variations are almost infinite. It carried on the legacy that had come over from Greece and Rome, through Gaul, and the Ancient British coinage. A head or a bust, intended to be that of the ruler in most cases, often appears on the obverse. This is usually surrounded by a legend, frequently the King's name. The reverse often contains a cross, which takes various forms, sometimes highly decorated, though it is by no means the standard reverse type. Where it is used there is usually a circle round it, with a circular legend between this circle and the outer edge of the coin. This is where the names of the moneyer and of the town usually occur.

A point of interest about the designs as a whole is that, during this period, they are put together by the use of a number of punches, not so far removed from the broken nail idea mentioned in an earlier chapter. By now the broken nail has become a punch, usually referred to as an iron. A collection of such punches, with straight or curved lines, small circles, dots, complete letters or parts thereof, formed a moneyer's 'alphabet'. With them he could build up a face and lettering for the legend, together with numerous 'decorations' for the various parts of the coin. As technique progressed a whole face might be engraved on a single punch, or a whole letter or a complete legend, though this is looking far ahead.

The Penny, such as has been described, was the sole coin in use in England for some five hundred years. Halfpennies and Farthings were obtained, over a long period,

92 *Gold Sovereign (obv.) of Henry VIII, third coinage.*

93 *Gold Sovereign (obv.) of Edward VI, second coinage. In this reign gold, having been reduced in fineness by Henry VIII, was raised from 20 to 23 carats.*

94 *The silver Crown was introduced in Edward VI's reign—this piece is dated 1551 (obv.).*

95, 96 *Silver Groat of Mary's reign (95), and a silver Shilling of Philip and Mary (obvs.).*

97 a, b *An Elizabeth I gold Sovereign. The fineness of the coinage was now at last restored.*

98 *Besieged towns and castles in the Civil War produced their own 'siege' money, such as this gold piece from Colchester.*

99 *Charles I's Oxford Crown.*

97 a

97 b

98

99

by cutting the Penny into halves and quarters, an unsatisfactory method which led to many abuses, as any tampering with a coin always will. This long period takes us out of Anglo-Saxon England into Norman England. William I, called the Conqueror (1066–87), took over the established Penny coinage, and it was continued till the accession of the fifth Plantagenet King, Edward I (1272–1307).

With the accession of Edward I English coinage began to expand. Of first importance was the striking of round Halfpennies and Farthings and the abolition of the practice of cutting Pennies into smaller pieces. To this range of three coins a fourth was now added, though numismatists regard it as experimental. This was the Groat or great piece, value fourpence, almost as thin as the Penny but as large as a modern Florin. The impact of this new coin on the economic situation is not known. What is known is that most of the pieces that have survived are gilded and appear to have been worn as jewellery (coins as 'costume jewellery' is not a new idea). No Groats were struck during the reign of Edward II (1307–27) and it was left to Edward III (1327–77) really to expand the coinage.

By 1344 an economic crisis (these are not new either!) caused the ordering of a new coinage. Gold was coined for the first time since the seventh century, apart from a few rare and probably experimental gold pieces of Henry III. The first gold piece to be struck was the Florin, taking its name from a Florentine piece of the same name, with its half and quarter. Because the Florin, valued at 6s, twice that of the Italian piece, was wrongly valued against silver coinage, it was struck only from January to August 1344. Its place was taken by the gold Noble, value 6s 8d, with a Half- and a Quarter-noble.

The gold Noble was a fine coin, showing the King standing in a ship, possibly inspired as a design by the naval victory of Sluys, 1340; for this is the period of the wars with France, Edward the Black Prince and the victories of Crécy and Poitiers – together with the defeats, not so frequently referred to.

The new coinage of Edward III finally settled into: in gold, Noble, Half-noble, Quarter-noble; in silver,

100, 101   *Two studies of Elizabeth I –on the obverse of a milled gold Half-pound piece (100), and on an official seal.*

Groat, Half-groat, Penny, Halfpenny and Farthing. This range continued in use till the first reign of Edward IV (1461–70). The Half and Quarter-nobles then ceased to be struck. In 1464–5 a Ryal or Rose-noble worth 10s took the Noble's place, under another coinage reorganization designed to attract gold to the English mint. Since 6s 8d, the value of the Noble, had become the standard charge for certain professional services—and still remained well into the twentieth century—a gold Angel of this value was struck. By the restoration of Henry VI (October 1470–April 1471)—this is the period of the main part of the Wars of the Roses—the Angel and Half-angel were the only gold coins struck. These two continued till the reign of Henry VII (1485–1509) when the Sovereign made its first appearance as an English coin and the Ryal made a brief reappearance.

The reign of Henry VIII (1509–47) started with a gold coinage of a Sovereign, Angel and Half-angel, but once more an economic crisis brought forth the need for English coinage to be realigned with that of the Continent, and Cardinal Wolsey was given the work in 1526. His measures provided, between 1526 and 1544, a gold coinage consisting of a Sovereign, Angel, Half-angel, George Noble, Half George Noble, Crown of the Rose, Crown of the Double Rose and a Halfcrown. Most of these pieces are extremely rare and during this adjustment the metal content of some of the coins was slightly reduced, from 23 to 22 carats and finally 20 carats. After 1544 the gold denominations were Sovereign, Half-sovereign, Angel, Half-angel, Quarter-angel, Crown and Halfcrown. In the meantime the silver coins, which had been going quietly along with their five denominations, were now debased and had a piece called a Testoon or Shilling added to them. This is the famous piece from which the ageing King's ample features look straight out from a coin made of such debased silver that the copper soon showed through, earning for the monarch the name of 'Old Coppernose'. This debasement of the coinage had been brought about by a further financial crisis, engendered by Henry having spent both the large fortune left to him by his father and all that he could obtain by other means.

In passing it should be mentioned that a Testoon was struck during the previous reign, that of Henry VII (1485–1509), though this piece is now regarded as a tentative issue. What is of interest about the piece is that for the first time for many centuries an actual profile portrait of the King appeared, thus starting a custom still in being. Similar portraits appeared on some of the Groats and Half-groats, and were the work of one Alexander de Brugsal—the name is variously spelt—who created the ancestors of our modern portrait coinage. Brugsal is also famous for his artistic treatment of the wholly medieval design of the Sovereign of Henry VII.

The short reign of Edward VI (1547–53), Henry VIII's only male child, saw the beginning of a long struggle to get the coinage back on firm ground once more. During the early years of the reign base coinage continued to be struck, some of it with the name and portrait of Henry VIII still on it. In 1549 gold was coined at 22 carats and later reached 23 carats again, both being used at once for a period. Silver was improved and the reign saw the introduction of a silver Crown, Halfcrown, Shilling and Sixpence which were the direct ancestors of Britain's present series of these names (fast disappearing, however, with the adoption of the decimal system).

The reign of Mary (1553–4) and Philip and Mary (1554–8) saw a continuation of improvement in the coinage, though some base pieces continued to be struck. It was not till the reign of Elizabeth I (1558–1603) that the fineness of the coinage was ultimately restored. Some of the coins of the previous reign showed Philip and Mary face to face, the only coinage in the British series where such a design is used.

Some tentative experiments with milled coins were undertaken during Elizabeth I's reign, but came to nothing. Dates, which first appeared in the reign of Edward VI, now began increasingly to be part of the coin's design, arabic and occasionally roman figures being used. This started the displacement of mint marks as such, which, in their original form, finally disappeared in

102

103

102, 103 *In James I's reign : Rose-ryal and Laurel. The laurel wreath of the latter strives to give the King the appearance of a Roman Emperor (obvs.).*

the reign of Charles II (1660–85). They were revived for a short time, though not quite in their ancient form, during the recoinage of William III (1694–1702) when provincial mints functioned briefly.

Mint marks proper were usually in the form of a small object, such as a lion, a lis, a rose, an acorn or an animal's head. At various times they signified either where the coin was struck, who struck it or on whose behalf it was struck, or the period or date during which the coin was struck. Thus a castle on the coins of Elizabeth I signifies that the pieces so marked were struck during the period 1570–2. The period during which any one mint mark was used varies, for a number of reasons, during the hammered coinage period.

Hammered coinage in gold and silver continued in use during the reign of James I (1603–25). The gold issues were complicated by the introduction or revival of such pieces as the Rose-ryal, Spur-ryal, Angel, Half-angel, Unite (signifying the union of the thrones of England and Scotland, since James reigned over both countries), Double-crown, Britain Crown, Thistle Crown, Halfcrown, Laurel and Half- and Quarter-laurel. The latter pieces showed James wearing a laurel wreath and trying to look like a Roman Emperor. An issue of copper Farthings, made under licence, was started during the reign in an attempt to provide much-needed small change. Though the King and various licensees made a handsome profit from the idea, few others did and the pieces were extensively forged. No further attempts to produce milled coins were undertaken during the reign.

The troubled reign of Charles I (1625–49) produced a coinage of the highest numismatic interest as soon as the Civil War broke out. The whole period is worthy of a book on its own but space will allow only the briefest mention here. The Tower Mint, the only one then in use, was lost to the King as soon as the war started. A branch mint had been set up at Aberystwyth under Sir Thomas Bushell to make use of locally mined silver. This was moved to Shrewsbury, and during the course of the war mints operated for the King at York, Coombe Martin (possibly), Oxford, Bristol, Truro, Exeter, Weymouth and/or

Sandsfoot Castle, Worcester and Chester; while the besieged towns or castles of Carlisle, Scarborough, Pontefract, Newark and Colchester issued their own roughly produced siege money. The Tower Mint continued to issue coins showing the King on them, that they might be accepted, and Nicholas Briot, who had come over from Paris, continued some experiments with milled coins but, probably mainly due to the war, the system was still not adopted.

Under the Commonwealth (1649–60) hammered coins in gold and silver still continued, the design, by Thomas Simon, being plain in the extreme. A series of milled coins was produced showing Cromwell's head but the Protector died before they went into use.

To bridge the gap from 1660 till 1662 a hammered coinage was issued during the reign of Charles II (1660–85) but the stage was being set for a complete reform in minting methods, the rearrangement of the gold denominations and the start of a series of coins which are the direct ancestors of British milled coinage as used till 1971. This will be dealt with in later chapters.

104

105

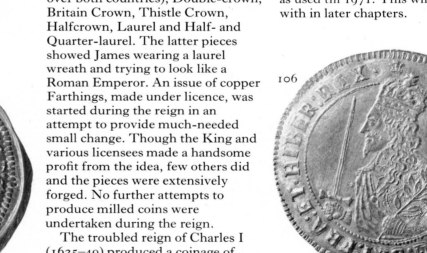

106

107

110 c

108 a

110 a

111

108 b

110 b

104, 105, 106, 107, 108 a, b
*Examples of Charles I's coinage : an
eight-sided silver Shilling, used as a
siege piece at Pontefract (104) (obv.) ;
a silver Halfcrown (obv.) probably
struck at Hartlebury Castle, at a time
when a war mint operated from
Worcester (105) ; a gold Triple Unite
struck at the Oxford mint in 1644
(106) ; and two examples of Briot's
experimental milled coinage—a silver
Halfcrown (107) (obv.), and a gold
Unite or 20 Shilling piece by the same
artist (108 a, b).*

109   *A Commonwealth gold Unite,
with a plain design by Thomas Simon.*

110 a, b, c   *A series of milled coins,
showing the Protector's head, appeared
briefly until his death—the bust is
comparable to the wax portrait (110c).*

111   *Charles II gold Unite—
hammered coins such as this were
soon to be abandoned as new minting
methods appeared and milled coinage
was issued.*

109

THE COIN REACHES AMERICA

112 a, b   *An 8 Reale piece, struck in Mexico in 1651, and known as a 'Cob' piece.*

In looking at the coinage development in America we are dealing for the first time with an area of which the coinage did not develop directly from Roman origins. By the time Europeans made the permanent discovery of America—it had undoubtedly been visited by the Norsemen *circa* AD 1000 and, according to some schools of thought, by the Chinese—the coinage brought to America came from settled monetary systems now long past the shadow of departed Rome.

It hardly needs repeating that the Spaniards in their explorations and military occupation in the central American regions found incalculable wealth in gold and silver, particularly in Mexico and Peru. To deal with part of this, mints were set up in such places as Lima, Guatemala, Mexico, Potosi, Santa Fe and Santiago. Here the metal was struck into coin and sent to Europe and Asia via the Pacific route. Here began all those stories, real and imaginary, of 'Pieces of Eight', with piratical actions at sea as violent as any in fiction.

Some of the earliest pieces struck in Spanish America go back as far as 1555, so that it can be said that, while the Spaniards took money with them to America in the first instance, the coin reached America as an export rather than an import.

A word or two ought perhaps to be said here about the large imports into Europe and Asia of the gold and silver mined in Spanish America. The defeat of the Spanish Armada in 1588, though it saved Britain from Spanish domination, neither killed Spanish power nor bankrupted Spain. The plate fleets still continued to sail, east and west, from America and were still attacked by Britain and the pirates. Thus in 1703 we find English coins struck with the word VIGO under the bust of Queen Anne, recording

the capture of bullion at the Battle of Vigo Bay. In 1746 we find British coins with LIMA under the bust of George II, recording the capture by Admiral Anson of a plate ship in the Philippines and the capture by other piratical ships of bullion from the Atlantic plate fleets. In 1804 we find Spanish Eight Reale pieces being countermarked with the head of George III for use in Britain and similar pieces being planed flat and restruck as Bank of England Dollars. It was not till the Spanish military occupation and direct influence in America was gradually brought down, by war and civil strife and by many of the South American countries attaining self-government (cf. Bolivar 'the liberator'), that the flow of Spanish gold and silver in its original form was brought to an end.

In North America, in the territories now known as the United States and Canada, coin was imported rather than exported. It has to be remembered that, at the outset of the opening up and colonization of this area, Russia, Britain, Sweden, Holland and France all held various areas, with Spain holding Mexico, 'south of the border', and California. The Russians sold their claim, Alaska, to the United States in 1867, the French sold Louisiana in 1803, the British conquered Canada from the French and were themselves driven out of the American colonies after the Declaration of Independence (1776), 1782 being the year that independence was recognized. We can look, then, for various coinages being imported into or struck in the North American continent while all this evolution was proceeding.

At first the early New England settlers carried on the fur trade with the Indians by the use of a commodity called wampum. This was made of shells in the form of beads. Wampum, beaver skins and

113, 114 *Working a silver mine in Potosi. The Spaniards found immense wealth in the gold and silver deposits of the American continent, and shipped their treasure away in their silver fleets.*

Virginian tobacco soon became the accepted form of currency. Though the immigrants had little or no use for coined money the arrival of traders soon gave rise to the demands for payment in coin. Almost any foreign coin was accepted, French, English, German, Dutch and Spanish, usually in the larger denominations such as Guineas and Spanish Eight Reales. From this last came eventually the American Dollar as a large silver coin, but the Spanish piece remained as a standard unit not only throughout the entire colonial period but was still circulating with official sanction as late as 1857.

As was so often to be the case the British government ignored the monetary plight of the colonists and made no effort to provide them with money in either large or small denominations. Thus it came about that the first coins minted in what was to become the United States were struck by John Hull in the Massachusetts Bay Colony. Having been authorized by the General Court of the colony the Boston mint struck the first metallic currency in the English Americas in 1652. These pieces consisted of plain, roughly circular flans of silver, made from bullion obtained from the West Indies. The obverse simply had N E in script lettering and the reverse XII (Shilling), VI (Sixpence), or III (Threepence) stamped at the top of the flan. (N E of course stood for New England.) All these pieces are now of the greatest rarity, only two of the Threepences being known as still in existence.

Naturally such simple pieces invited forgery and clipping, so a better designed piece had to be evolved. Two types were struck, known as the Willow Tree and Oak Tree pieces, so called on account of the tree which occupied the centre of the obverse in each type. The tree was enclosed in a ring of dots, outside which was the legend MASATHVSETS IN, variously arranged. In the centre of the reverse was the date, 1652, and the value XII, VI or III as appropriate, with the legend NEW ENGLAND AN DOM, again variously arranged. Once more the pieces were roughly produced by the hammer and were quickly forged. A whole treatise has been written on these pieces and their forgeries in order to help

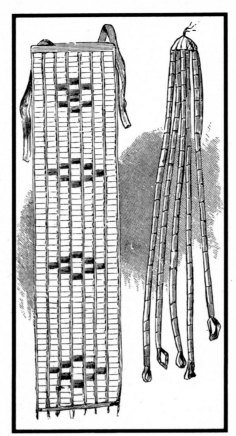

115 *Wampum belt and strings. Wampum, together with beaver skins and tobacco, was the accepted form of currency between the North American Indians and the early settlers.*

116 a, b *Massachusetts Oak Tree Shilling, 1652. The 'tree' coins were all dated 1652, even though minted several years later.*

117 a, b *English Halfpenny, 1772.*

118 a, b *Rosa Americana Twopence, 1723.*

collectors sort out the true from the false. All the pieces are dated 1652 but they were struck for about thirty years without the date being changed, the reason being that Charles II disapproved of the issues. It was better not to let him know that the pieces were still being struck! All these are again very rare coins. They were followed by the Pine Tree series, similar pieces but with a different tree. These were also dated 1652 and had the same denominational values, but were actually struck between 1667 and 1682. They are not so rare as the two preceding types and are again subject to many forgeries.

Next comes Maryland, where in 1658 Cecil, second Lord Baltimore, began to issue silver Shillings, Sixpences and Fourpences and a copper Penny. They had his head, to right, on the obverse and the three silver pieces had the Baltimore arms on the reverse. All are now of great rarity.

A certain Mark Newby arrived in New Jersey from Ireland in 1681 and brought with him some Halfpennies said to have been struck in Dublin in 1678. These pieces, known as St Patrick Halfpence, since they depicted the Saint on them, were soon widely used and were authorized as legal tender in New Jersey Province in 1682. Similar Farthings were also put into use.

Next followed a prolific issue by William Wood, an Englishman who had obtained a patent, or licence, from George I to make copper tokens for Ireland and the American colonies. Some of the pieces are undated while others are dated 1722, 1723, 1724 and 1733 respectively.

On 12 July 1722, Wood also obtained a patent to strike coins for 'The Plantations' as the American colonies were then known, for a term of fourteen years. The metal of which these coins were made was known as 'Bath metal'. Twenty ounces of it were made up of 1 pennyweight of silver, 4 oz. 19 dwt. of tutanaigne and 15 oz. of brass. (Tutanaigne is a white alloy of copper, zinc or spelter, and originated in China or the West Indies.) In this metal Wood struck coins now known as the 'Rosa Americana' series, from the large full-blown rose that appeared on the reverse. They were issued during this period from dies engraved by Lammas, Harold and Stanbroke, and were struck at the French Change, Hogg Lane, Seven Dials, London.

When first struck the pieces were in high relief, with a brassy-gold appearance which soon wore off, as did the high relief. Struck hot, many examples appeared blistered and the softness of the metal probably accounts for the fact that few pieces which survive are in really fine condition. The denominations were Twopence, Penny and Halfpenny, some undated, with the head of George I to right, on the obverse. They are all now rare, especially in anything approaching fine condition. Some of Wood's Irish coinage, briefly mentioned, also found their way to North America and are also quite rare pieces.

This was the end of the series of coins sometimes known collectively as the 'Plantation Pieces'. Following the Declaration of Independence, 1776, officially recognized by Britain in 1782, the one-time colonies were not slow to take in hand the matter of providing money. New Hampshire was the first state to consider the matter, but although patterns for coins were prepared in 1776 little of the proposed coinage was ever put into circulation. Vermont was first off the mark, permission being granted to Reuben Harmon to coin copper pieces in June 1785. Between that year and 1788 there were struck the now-famous series of Vermont Cents, of which the eleven varieties are all now rare, some being unobtainable. Strangely enough some of the 1787 and 1788 pieces had the head of George III on the obverse and Britannia on the reverse. Some of the 1788 pieces even had the legend GEORGIUS III REX, though there was now no official connection with Britain.

In New York in 1787 a partnership of ten individuals set up a 'manufactory of hardware', and from this came a series of copper coins, the operations being conducted in secret and the products looked upon as illegal. Two of the partners, Harmon and Cooley, were listed as co-partners 'in such trades and merchandizing and in the coinage of copper for the states of Vermont, Connecticut and New York, for their most benefit advantage and profit'.[1]

'Perhaps many of the pieces now classified as Connecticut coins, the Vermont Auctori with the Britannia reverse and the counterfeit George III Halfpence, were products of this "hardware manufactory".'[2]

In Connecticut itself authority to establish a mint was granted to two private individuals in 1785, and the French colonies—then Louisiana so far as the 'United States' was concerned—had pieces struck at Rouen and Rochelle in circulation. There were many other pieces still to be struck in various parts of the United States before the whole situation was regularized and the United States coinage emerged.

There was quite a large number of miscellaneous pieces, many of them tokens and frequently rare, struck before United States coinage settled into a pattern. Even then a few token or private pieces appeared as late as the 1790s.

A considerable amount of work had to be done and a great deal of consideration given to the whole matter of a coinage for the United States. The Spanish Dollar, or Eight Reales, and its subdivisions appear to have been the coins most familiar among the general coinage confusion. Gouverneur Morris, the Assistant Financier of the Confederation, proposed a decimal coinage ratio and on this proposal Robert Morris, Superintendent of Finance, issued a report to Congress in January 1782. The unit Morris proposed was 1/1440 of a Dollar, since this was calculated to agree with all the different valuations at which the Spanish Dollar was taken in the various states. Plans for a mint were formulated and a government mint was proposed in February 1782, but no further steps were taken at that time.

During 1784 Jefferson, in his capacity as a member of the House of Representatives, submitted a further report which disagreed with Morris's suggested unit on the grounds that it was too complicated. Jefferson favoured a decimal system—as opposed to a decimal ratio with the Spanish Dollar—pointing out that 'the most easy ratio of multiplication and division is that of ten'.

[1] Yeoman, *A Guide Book of United States Coins*
[2] Ibid.

116 a

116 b

117 a

117 b

118 a

118 b

119   *The signing of the Declaration of Independence, 4 July 1776.*

120 a, b   *Large Cent 1794.*

121 a, b   *Large 1855 Cent piece.*

122 a, b   *1859 Cent piece with Indian head.*

123 a, b, c   *Buffalo, or Indian head, Nickel issued between 1913-38, and replaced by the Jefferson type Nickel (123c) which established the use of portraits rather than of symbolic devices.*

124 a, b   *Franklin D. Roosevelt on the Dime (1946) with the initials of John Sinnock, the designer, at the truncation of the neck.*

125 a, b   *1916 Standing Liberty type Quarter Dollar, a rare coin as the reverse design was modified the following year.*

123 a

123 b

123 c

121 a

124 a

124 b

120 a

120 b

125 a

125 b

126 a, b *The Kennedy Half Dollar issued in 1964.*

127 a, b *The Peace Dollar, struck in 1921 and put into circulation early in 1922.*

128 a, b *An 1808 Quarter Eagle. Previous to this year the bust on the obverse had faced right and been capless.*

129 a, b *2½ Dollar Gold piece of 1913, of a type first issued in 1908 that departed from all preceding types in the United States series.*

126 a

126 b

127 a

127 b

128 a

128 b

129 a

129 b

In May 1785 the Grand Committee recommended a gold Five-dollar piece, a silver Dollar with subdivisions, in silver, of one-half, one-quarter, one-tenth and one-twentieth of a Dollar, with copper pieces of one-hundredth and one-two-hundredth of a Dollar. Formal approval was given by Congress in July 1785, but nothing further could be done at that time owing to the state of affairs in the country. Meanwhile Massachusetts struck Cents and Half-cents in 1787 and 1788, which were the first official coins to have a stated value as decimal parts of the Dollar unit, the Cent being one-hundredth part of the Dollar. The first federally authorized coin was the Fugio or Franklin Cent, which was struck privately under contract with the Government in 1787.

A further report, that of Alexander Hamilton, Secretary of the Treasury, appeared in January 1791. It agreed in all essentials with the decimal Dollar system and the use of bi-metallic currency. Finally, in April 1792, came the passing of a Bill which provided 'that the money of account of the United States should be expressed in Dollars or units, Dismes or tenths, Cents or hundredths and Milles or thousandths; a Disme being the tenth part of a Dollar, a Cent the hundredth part of a Dollar, a Mille the thousandth part of a Dollar'.[1]

Thus the coinage of the United States of America came into being, basically against much the same background as the establishment of most other major coinages. The range of coinage set up was as follows:

Gold
   Eagle, value $10
   Half-eagle = $5
   Quarter-eagle = $2·50
Silver
   Dollar = $1
   Half-dollar = 50 Cents
   Quarter-dollar = 25 Cents
   Disme (soon Dime) = 10 Cents
   Half-disme = 5 Cents
Copper
   Cent = ·01 of a Dollar
   Half-cent = ·005 of a Dollar

In July 1792, the actual building of the mint was started on Seventh Street, Philadelphia, and the

---

[1] Yeoman, op. cit.

71

130, 131   *The rough with the smooth.*
The sedate interior of the Philadelphia
mint as contrasted with the frenetic
activities in the California gold mines.

132   *David Rittenhouse, who*
organized the first US mint
in Philadelphia and served as its
Director from 1792-95.

133   *The American Numismatic*
Society.

132

133

73

134

135 b

134   *Obverse of a 1795 Silver Dollar.*

135 a, b   *Massachusetts Pine Tree Shilling with the familiar date of 1652 on it.*

136 a, b *Large Canadian Cent 1876, the first year that 'Dominion' large cents were issued. All Canadian coins were minted in England until 1908.*

136 a

136 b

well-known philosopher and scientist, David Rittenhouse, was appointed by Washington as its first Director. In the course of time other mints were needed in the United States, just as many mints had come into being and been finally eliminated in Britain. There are, or have been, mints at Charlotte, North Carolina; Carson City, Nevada; Dahlonega, Georgia; Denver, Colorado; New Orleans, Louisiana; Philadelphia, Pennsylvania; and San Francisco, California.

Canada

A word must be said about Canadian coinage in this brief survey of the coin reaching America. Even so this will leave the whole of South America out of the story, though the present countries there are of somewhat later formation.

The attempts after the Peace of Paris in 1763 to introduce British institutions into Canada led to friction. This was not entirely allayed by the Quebec Act of 1774 (George III), which secured the religious and civil rights of the French in Canada and annexed to Quebec parts of Minnesota, Wisconsin, Michigan, Ohio, Indiana and Illinois. These passed from Britain again in 1783. By 1791 Quebec had been divided into Upper and Lower Canada. This proving unsatisfactory and leading to rebellion in 1837–8 (Victoria), the two provinces were reunited in 1840, though this also was not a success. Things were moving towards a settlement, however, as far back as 1770. In that year St John Island (renamed Prince Edward Island in 1780), and in 1784 New Brunswick, were formed out of Nova Scotia into separate colonies. In 1858 British Columbia was made a Crown Colony, owing to an influx of population caused by a gold rush. Vancouver Island was joined to it in 1866, while in 1864 the maritime provinces had under discussion possible local confederation. The chance was then taken to discuss a broad scheme to cover all British North America and the basis of union agreed on resulted in the formation of the Dominion of Canada in 1867. Finally Newfoundland joined this confederation in 1949.

The coinage of the French régime was followed by a prolific issue of tokens, mainly on a

137 a, b *The 1939 issue of the Canadian Silver Dollar was commemorative of the visit to Canada of King George VI and Queen Elizabeth. The reverse shows the Parliament Building in Ottawa.*

138 a, b *Edward VII Canadian 50 Cents piece 1904.*

139 a, b *1937 10 Cents piece, the first year that the fishing schooner appeared on the reverse.*

140 a, b *Twelve-sided 5 Cents piece of 1944. In the centre of the reverse design are a torch and Sir Winston Churchill's V for Victory sign. The dots and dashes round the border represent Morse code for 'We win when we work willingly'.*

141 a, b *When George VI came to the throne, the proclamation for the new Nickel specified '5 cents between two maple leaves and a beaver'.*

137 a

137 b

138 a

138 b

139 a

139 b

140 a

140 b

141 a

141 b

provincial basis. These lasted well into the reign of Queen Victoria (1837–1901), some being on the decimal and some on the sterling basis. These were issued mostly by banks and trading companies. A considerable improvement in the coinage took place after the reunion of Upper and Lower Canada. English and American gold and silver were in use, copper being supplied by the Bank of Montreal (1842 and 1844), the Quebec Bank (1852), and the Bank of Upper Canada between 1850 and 1857. The decimal system was finally adopted in 1858, the unit being the Dollar, then equivalent to that of the United States. What can be considered as Canadian coinage proper began in 1870. Silver was issued locally and English and American silver taken out of circulation. In 1876 Cents were struck, though British Halfpennies were taken as Cents till enough of the former could be provided. The bank coppers and those of New Brunswick and Nova Scotia were also allowed to continue in use and it was not till about 1900 that the

Canadian coinage became uniform throughout the Dominion.

Gold ten and five Dollars appeared in 1912 but the issue was never prolific and ceased in 1914. British Sovereigns, with a letter C as mint mark, were struck in Canada, and are dated between 1908 and 1919. The desirability of a gold coinage for Canada led to the establishment of a branch of the Royal Mint in Ottawa, and it is from this mint that the Sovereigns with mint mark C came, as well as the ten and five Dollars of local design. This establishment is now the Royal Canadian Mint.

The range of Canadian coins at its fullest extent comprised ten and five Dollars in gold, Sovereign in gold, and Dollar, Half-dollar, Quarter-dollar, ten Cents, five Cents in silver, nickel, tombac and steel (as wartime measures) and Cents in bronze. Not being tied too closely to British coin design tradition, many fine imaginative pieces have appeared, especially in late years; although they have always had on the obverse the head of the British monarch.

142 a, b, c   *Eagles, $10 Gold Pieces.
The small eagle reverse was only used
until 1797 and is therefore rare. It
was replaced by the larger heraldic
eagle. The obverse of the 1801 coin
shows a pattern of 8 stars Left and 5
Right. Around this time these
patterns were extremely variable.*

143 a, b   *A 1908 Double Eagle or
$20 gold piece, the largest coin among
the regular United States issues. This
one is of the Saint-Gaudens type,
which originally had the date in
Roman numerals and no motto. Here
the date is in Arabic numerals and the
motto 'In God We Trust' has been
added.*

142 a

142 b

142 c

143 a

144 a, b   *The Four-Dollar Gold, or 'Stella'. The gold coins were only struck in 1879 and 1880, and fell into two distinct types, one showing a lady with flowing hair, as here, and the other showing the same lady with coiled hair.*

145 a, b   *Canada opened a branch of the Royal Mint in Ottawa early in the 1900s, and began to strike her own gold coinage. $5 and $10 gold pieces, such as this one of 1912, were struck in that year and in 1913, 1914.*

144 a

144 b

145 a

145 b

143 b

THE COIN REACHES AUSTRALASIA

It is an odd twist of history that the coin reached Australia before Australia was, officially, discovered. Perhaps a word of explanation is needed. As a mixture of races Europeans are fond of setting down the date when they discovered America, Australia, and so forth, only to find in most cases that someone had found the place before. So far as Australia is concerned, the precise date at which this, the largest island on the Earth's surface, was discovered is not known, but it is asserted that Magellan's followers sighted western Australia in 1552. It would seem probable, however, that this island, into which most of Europe could be put and almost lost, was discovered long before that date.

To the north lies the eastern end of Asia—China—and south of China are the long Malayan peninsula and the vast archipelago of islands forming the East Indies. In this great area many of the people were maritime traders, sailing between the mainland and the multitude of islands. Many of these traders travelled in small ships, but the Chinese junks were often of larger, more solid construction, capable of long voyages, well crewed and excellently navigated.

While the Europeans were busy inventing coinage, China, according to its ancient authorities, had a metallic coinage as early as the twentieth century BC. It is not beyond the bounds of possibility, therefore, that the Chinese traders and adventurers, not to mention the traders sailing through the massive archipelago to the south of China, knew of Australia. The Far Eastern peoples had no use for this uninhabited region. It was left neglected, but those who happened there probably had some form of metallic currency with them, though there was no use for it so far as Australia was concerned.

146 *Long before Australia was officially 'discovered', the seas of that hemisphere were peopled by maritime traders such as this boatload from China or Java, who presumably knew of the Australian continent.*

147 a

147 b

147 a, b   *William IV gold 2 Mohurs of 1835, issued by the East India Company, and one of a number of alien coins that came into use in Australia in the course of trade.*

148 The largest gold coin in the world, a 200 Mohur piece of 1654, shown here in its actual size—5·3 inches in diameter. Unfortunately the coin has been lost, but the British Museum has a cast of it.

148

149 An 'Adelaide Ingot', one of the legal gold tokens that were used as a temporary measure after the Australian Gold Rush when coin was scarce. Most of these were later melted down, so the survivors are rare and valuable.

149

150 *The Dutch as mercantile traders built up a commercial empire that meant coin was distributed around the globe.*

151 *Ships at anchor in Botany Bay.*

152

154

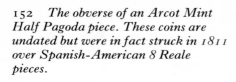

153

155

152   *The obverse of an Arcot Mint Half Pagoda piece. These coins are undated but were in fact struck in 1811 over Spanish-American 8 Reale pieces.*

153, 154   *Early seventeenth-century Hindustan Mohur, showing on the obverse the turbaned bust of the emperor with a goblet held in front of the face, and on the reverse a lion beneath a radiate sun.*

155   *Hyderabad Mohur (obv.), late nineteenth or early twentieth century, showing Persian style minaret or mosque.*

The Dutch East India Company, that great rival of the English Company of the same name, had been trading with the Far East—Malaya and the archipelago—since the sixteenth century. The course which their vessels eventually took from Africa crossed the Indian Ocean far to the south in a straight line from the Cape, and a turn north was made when land was sighted. This land was the west coast of Australia. Here some of the ships ran into trouble and were wrecked, some of them carrying chests of coin to be used in the East Indian trade. The writer has had one such piece in his pocket for many years. It came from the *Gilt Dragon,* a Dutch ship from Amsterdam which went down off the west coast of Australia before Australia was known as a country. Those who survived such wrecks and got ashore, possibly with coins in their possession, are supposed to have attempted to survive inland and finally to have been lost in this vast, empty island-continent. It is probable, therefore, that 'the coin' reached Australia when the various small parts of its coast that were known to Europeans were no more than question-marks on the maritime maps of the world.

Ever since coins were invented, those who went to live in new countries all over the world had no more money than that which they carried with them. As settlements developed—the first civilized settlement in Australia was made at Botany Bay in 1788—and trade with other countries began, any reasonable form of money which the traders brought with them came to be accepted. Foremost among such coins, in Australia as elsewhere, was the Spanish Dollar. Before the usual miscellaneous selection of the world's coins came into use, however, there was much confusion. A quotation from the work of Coleman P. Hyman, *An Account of the Coins, Coinages and Currency of Australia,* 1893, will give some idea of this confusion.

'While it is discouraging to find that the majority of writers on early Australian affairs pass over the matter of coins and currency without any reference, every established fact tends to show that though a very small amount of English money was used during the first few years after the arrival of "the first fleet", the majority of the dealings were arranged by barter: rum, corn, and other marketable produce being in high favour for the purpose of settling claims, Dollars also being recognized. The first form of Barter between the settlers and the natives appears (according to Governor Phillip's journal) [Captain Arthur Phillip, R.N., the first Governor] to have been established at Parramatta in 1791, the settlers giving small quantities of rice or bread in exchange for fish, of which the natives frequently caught more than they required for immediate use.

'During September 1791', some transports arrived and 'several articles of Comfort were introduced' but 'the Spanish Dollar was the current coin of the Colony, which some masters taking at 5s, others at 4s 6d, the Governor in consideration of the officers, having been obliged to receive it at 5s *sterling*, issued a proclamation fixing the currency of the Spanish Dollar at that sum'.

Continuing the story Hyman writes: 'It may well be said the rummiest currency known was that initiated here when rum came to be so extensively used as a circulating medium. At first tacitly recognized by the authorities, in a few years this currency became a curse almost ineradicable; Governor Hunter forbade the bartering of spirits for grain, but, like many other orders, these were unheeded.'

It might be pointed out here that Australia was not alone in the use of spirits as a form of currency. In Africa gin was at one time a form of money. Bottles and cases were used in trade, often unopened, the full bottles passing from hand to hand.

As is always the case where an inadequate supply of coinage is encountered, forged coins soon come into being. Of the various pieces used in Australian trade, to be listed in a moment, forgeries soon appeared.

In 1800 an official announcement was published. It stated that English copper coin was to be issued for use in Australia and that the *Porpoise* was on its way with £550 of copper coinage. At this point it is interesting to detail a part of the announcement that listed other coins 'legally circulating in this Colony, with the Rates Affixed to each at which they shall be considered, and be legal tender in all payments or transactions in this Colony'. The list was as follows:

A Guinea	£1 2s 0d
A Johanna	£4 0s 0d
A Half-johanna	£2 0s 0d
A Ducat	9s 6d
A Gold Mohur	£1 17s 6d
A Pagoda	8s
A Spanish Dollar	5s
A Rupee	2s 6d
A Dutch Guilder	2s
An English Shilling	1s 1d
A Copper Coin of One Ounce	2d

The above list, while of interest in itself as showing something of the numerous coins in use in Australia in the course of trade, gives a side-light on the various nations trading with Australia. The Guinea, English Shilling and Copper Coin of One Ounce are British pieces. The Johanna comes from Portugal, as does its half. The Dutch Guilder comes from Holland; the trading ventures of the Dutch East India Company have already been mentioned. The Mohur, Pagoda and Rupee are of Indian origin while the Spanish Dollar was, as already mentioned, almost a universal coin.

Such English silver and gold coinage as was available in the colony was quite inadequate for requirements. The copper coinage brought by the *Porpoise* was speedily 'cornered'. There was just not enough money to go round. There was no money being struck in Australia. Something had to be done.

The near-universal Spanish Dollar was available in reasonable quantity. One of the first steps towards an Australian coinage was an attempt to convert this piece for local use. Governor Macquarie issued a proclamation dated 1 July 1813, which ordered that, as a quantity of Spanish Dollars had been sent in an attempt to help matters, these pieces should have a small central piece struck out of them. This piece should be impressed with the words NEW SOUTH WALES below a crown on the obverse, and FIFTEEN PENCE on the reverse. The little coin so formed was known as a Dump.

The part of the Spanish Dollar left after the Dump had been struck out of it formed a ring. This ring

156 a, b *New South Wales Holey Dollar.*

was stamped on its inner rim with the words FIVE SHILLINGS and a branch of laurel. On the opposite side the ring was stamped NEW SOUTH WALES 1813. This ring-piece became known as the Holey Dollar. Both pieces are now of great rarity.

This sort of temporary coinage gave rise at once to crops of forged pieces. Counterfeiting of Holey Dollars and Dumps reached such a state that by 1822 efforts were being made to withdraw them from use. By 1828 the Holey Dollar had fallen in exchange value to 3s 3d, and the Dump to 1s 1d. In 1829 both ceased to be current.

Meanwhile a certain amount of coin was still being sent out from London. It was quite inadequate in quantity for the growing needs of the colony. As a result – a result which always attends a shortage of money and small change – tokens began to appear.

Something over six hundred varieties of such token pieces were struck in or for Australia (and New Zealand, as will be seen), many of them in Britain. They served the threefold purpose of 'utility, profit and advertisement', since those who issued them put their names and style of business on them, as issuers of tokens always do. These token pieces continued in use till at least

1868. On 22 September in that year a Government Gazette Extraordinary announced that 'arrangements having now been completed for the distribution of the Imperial bronze coinage, the Colonial Treasurer directs the withdrawal of the Treasury notice of the 5 August last, under which, pending such arrangements, the copper tokens in circulation were to be taken in the ordinary transactions of business in the various public departments'.

As an added complication to economic matters in Australia, gold was discovered in 1851 in New South Wales and at the Victorian goldfields at Mount Alexander. By March 1852 over eight thousand men had left South Australia by sea and many more made the journey overland to the 'diggings', and as each 'digger' took with him as much ready cash as he could, about two-thirds of the available coin was lost. To add to these difficulties there were scarcely enough males left to get in the harvest: prices fell, property depreciated in value, transactions in cash became almost unknown and land and shares dropped to unheard-of low values. So much for the side-effects of a gold rush on a small population.

Something had to be done with the gold that was discovered. It was

157 *The first Australian Mint was opened in Sydney in 1855 in the south wing of the old rum hospital. It looked much the same in 1926 when it closed.*

158

158 *Reverse of a 1947 Fiji Threepence, showing a native hut.*

159 *Reverse of a George VI One Rupee nickel piece.*

of no use by itself. About £50,000 worth had arrived in the colony of New South Wales by January 1852. The scarcity of coin was such that merchants and bankers were forced to accept payment in gold dust at prices from about 56s to 70s per ounce. The obvious thing to do with the gold was to coin it, but this was at first rejected, being a direct violation of the Royal Prerogative. A loophole was found, however. The latest revised instructions to Governors of British Colonies 'prohibited assenting in Her Majesty's name to . . . Any Bill affecting the Currency of the Colony', but with the proviso 'unless urgent necessity exists requiring that such be brought into immediate operation'. Since such urgency certainly existed the South Australia Act of Parliament 1852 (no. 1) was rushed through all its stages in one day, and the first gold pieces struck for currency were issued in South Australia under authority of the first Bullion Act.

A small series of legal gold tokens now came into being. They consisted of thin plates of metal, some round, some roughly rectangular, bearing such legends as WEIGHT OF INGOT OZ. O DWT. 5 GR 8 EQUIVT. WEIGHT OF 22 CARATS OZ. O DWT. 5 GRS 15, with a crown

and the letters S.A. and 1 and 8 (= $\frac{1}{8}$) and 23 CARATS. These 'Adelaide Ingots', as they came to be known, are now pieces of the highest rarity. As a temporary measure they were not long in use and would, naturally, be melted down later. A few survive in museums and even fewer in private collections. One can be seen at the British Museum.

The next step was the repealing of the 1852 Act partly by the passing of another on 23 November. This authorized the Government Assayer at Adelaide, after he had assayed—tested the quality of—gold brought to him, to 'reduce the same to the fineness of standard gold, according to the standard of coined gold by the law of England and . . . thereafterwards cause the same to be divided into convenient portions, of the value, at the rate of Three Pounds Eleven Shillings per ounce of standard gold, of Five Pounds, Two Pounds, One Pound and Ten Shillings, as such Government Assayer may deem fit, and . . . stamp upon each portion the precise weight and value thereof, with such device as, being approved by the Governor, shall be published in the South Australian Gazette'. Such pieces were then deemed to be legal tender.

The battle was now half won. Something that could be used as money in a metal valuable enough to make reasonable transactions easy was about to be produced. Dies were prepared by the Adelaide Government Assay Office for the striking of gold coins of £5 and £1 in value. The design was quite simple, but not unpleasing in the result. In the centre of the obverse was the imperial crown above the date, 1852, and the whole was enclosed within a circle, made up of dots (beads) and a lacy type of decoration. In the space between this inner circle and the outer edge of the coin appeared the legend GOVERNMENT ASSAY OFFICE (a small rose as decoration) ADELAIDE (another similar rose). The reverse was similar. In the central compartment—the field— appeared the legend VALUE/ONE/ POUND in three lines. The perimeter legend read WEIGHT 5 DWT: 15 GRS (rose) 22 CARATS (rose). The battle was now won. Since these 'token' gold pieces bore no resemblance to the

160 *An octagonal coin with octave sides—King George V Four Annas, as struck in 1919, 1920, 1921.*

161 *A square coin with rounded corners—King George V Two Annas.*

162 *Obverse of 1895 British Trade Dollar. These coins were issued between 1895-1935 to promote British commerce in the East. They had been requested for many years by local bankers and merchants, who eventually paid the costs of their production.*

164

166

163

165

167

163 *Reverse of 1927 Australian Florin, struck to commemorate the opening of the Canberra Houses of Parliament.*

164 *Reverse of Edward VIII New Guinea Penny. All New Guinea coins have a hole in the centre.*

165 *Head of a merino sheep on the reverse of a 1941 Australian Shilling. No mint mark.*

166 *No mint mark again on the reverse of this 1943 Australian Penny.*

167 *Australia's attractive current coat-of-arms on the reverse of a 1945 Florin. No mint mark.*

Sovereign in their design, susceptibilities at Buckingham Palace and particularly in Whitehall had not been offended. Thus a growing and vigorous country got through a loophole. Unprovided with money by the government which had brought it into existence, it made its own.

As to the actual pieces themselves, none but restrikes of the £5 piece are known. A small number of the £1 pieces are still in existence and form very desirable pieces in the cabinets of collectors specializing in British and Commonwealth gold coins. As a matter of interest to the collector, after a reasonably large number of pieces had been struck the £1 die cracked. Striking continued from the damaged die, however, and pieces struck from it are more rare than those struck before the die cracked. The crack appears as a hair-line on the coins.

Thus we have the coin reaching Australia in various forms. Eventually branches of the Royal Mint in London were set up at Sydney (1853), Melbourne (1872) and Perth (1899), the main object being the coining of Sovereigns and a few Half-sovereigns from local gold, the design based on the London model but with the mint marks S, M and P respectively.

The main question of a coinage for Australia still remained open.

What had been provided was only on a local basis, to meet pressing needs. As communications improved, and as steamships began to replace sail on the ocean runs of the world, Australia was brought that much nearer to Britain. Imperial coinage began to reach Australia in greater amounts and was used there in conjunction with the coins then in use. This situation continued till the early 1920s but in the meantime a coinage for Australia was put in hand in the reign of Edward VII (1901–10). Florins, Shillings, Sixpences and Threepences were struck for Australia in 1910, but the death of the King brought this, the first official Australian coinage, to a premature end.

Now that it was official for Australia to have a coinage, production was continued in earnest during the next reign, that of George V (1910–36). To the denominations already listed above a Penny and Halfpenny of plain but not unpleasing design were added. The coinage for Australia, in silver and bronze, was struck at the Royal Mint in London, at the Calcutta (then branch) mint and at the mint of Ralph Heaton in Birmingham. This method of coin production was continued till 1918, from which date the branch mints of Sydney, Melbourne and Perth, founded to

168

168   The reverse of a 1935 New Zealand Crown, a commemorative coin struck partly in honour of the Silver Jubilee of George V. The obverse shows the crowned bust of the King, and the reverse depicts a naval captain and a Maori chief shaking hands, with WAITANGI inscribed below, recalling the treaty of that name which established British sovereignty over New Zealand in 1840.

169   A member of the Company of Captain Cook's ship Endeavour bartering a crayfish with a Maori. By an unknown artist.

169

deal with gold coinage, took over the main coin production.

Compared with the Imperial coinage, that of Australia at this period lacks two popular coins, the Halfcrown and the Farthing. Neither was ever struck in or for Australia, but in 1937 and again in 1938 a Crown was struck, though it had no half. Neither piece was popular in circulation, that of 1938 being the rarer. The first marked the coronation of George VI (1936–52), and was struck as a coin-medal (an almost unacceptable association of numismatic terms). As a commemorative piece Australia, quite rightly in the light of its coinage history, decided to use the Florin. Thus in 1927 Australia issued a commemorative Florin to mark the establishment of the Parliament at Canberra. Another followed to mark the centenary of Victoria and Melbourne, 1934–5. In 1951 a Florin commemorated the Jubilee of Australia, 1901–51, and in 1954 a further Florin commemorated the Royal Visit of Queen Elizabeth II.

To round off the story, the denominations listed above continued in use till Australia turned to decimal coinage in 1966. A brand new mint was opened at Canberra to deal with the new decimal coinage—just as a brand new Royal Mint has been set up in South Wales to deal with the same situation in Britain.

New Zealand

In New Zealand the beginnings of trade, both among the natives and with the Europeans when they arrived, took the familiar form of barter. At the time of the arrival of white men the Maori had not progressed beyond the Stone Age. Gold and other metals were unknown to him, though in places gold nuggets were lying around. The Maori had, however, become very skilful in fashioning stone, bone and wooden ornaments and weapons. Maoris were also excellent seamen and operated large fleets of sea-going canoes. Marauding expeditions were frequent but so far as trade was concerned the articles available for exchange were largely restricted to food, clothing (in the form of shoulder cloaks of flax and flax-woven waist garments not unlike kilts), and articles of warfare and adornment.

Something which was valued very highly among the Maori, representing almost what gold represented to the European, was greenstone. This the Maori fashioned into articles of adornment and use, and since the stone is difficult to come by and also difficult to work, the portable and very durable articles made from greenstone attained some of the status of money.

So far as money is concerned, the Maori began to prefer the use of coin in about 1835. Writing in that year, W. Yate in his *An Account of New Zealand* states: 'Barter of every description is now gradually giving way to the introduction of British coin and Dollars. One powerful reason why natives preferred money to blankets, clothing, arms and hardware, was that they were bound in honour to distribute it among their friends or, on the first cause of offence, to become dispossessed, but "gold and Dollars lie in so small a compass, that they can be easily concealed, or carried undiscovered about their persons", and parted with in small sums. "Counterfeit coin has been palmed upon them; medals have been passed for Dollars; and even gilded Farthings as Sovereigns." Usually they required a third person to vouch for the genuineness of the coin tendered.'

British Sovereignty was established in 1840 with the signing of the Treaty of Waitangi. Perhaps this was the greatest barter of all, since it bartered the sovereignty of the country for the advantages conferred by a powerful nation. To the Maori the interpretation of the treaty was 'The shadow of the land goes to the Queen; the substance remains with us'. The system of barter continued in use for a considerable period.

In the absence of British coinage, in part due to the remoteness of New Zealand from Britain, and in part to the unprecedented and deplorably bad condition of money supplies in Britain at the turn of the eighteenth and nineteenth centuries, the usual selection of various coinages was in use, including our old friend the Spanish Dollar. Amongst others, English, French and Indian coins were in use till 1847. A table not unlike that drawn up in Australia appeared in New Zealand, equating the various silver pieces to values in Shillings.

170 *The jade neck-ornaments known as Tikis which the Maoris fashioned with much skill.*

171 a

171 b

171 c

171 d

172

173 a

*171 a, b, c, d The reverses of
various George V New Zealand coins—
the crossed clubs on the Threepence,
the Huia bird on the Sixpence, the
Maori warrior on the Shilling, and the
Kiwi on the Florin.*

*172 The centennial Halfcrown
issued to commemorate the Treaty
of Waitangi. The figure in the centre is
a Maori woman.*

*173 a, b Contemporary sketches
from the days of the Australian Gold
Rush.*

The large crop of tokens struck
for use in Australia was mirrored
by similar issues for New Zealand.
In the main they were a picturesque
series, issued between 1857 and 1881
and withdrawn in 1897. The total
number of varieties recorded
was 147.

For ninety-three years British
Imperial coinage was the legal
metallic currency in New Zealand.
A local coinage was introduced in
1933, but even then this might not
have come about but for the
activities of smugglers during the
period 1930–3. During this period
the Australian Pound and later that
of New Zealand were progressively
depreciated against sterling.
Australian silver and bronze coins
had free but illegal circulation in
New Zealand and this gave the
coin-smugglers the chance to exploit
the exchange margin of both
countries when the exchange rate
varied. Matters were made worse
in 1933 when the New Zealand
Pound was artificially depreciated
in relation to sterling. The inflow
of Australian coins ceased but the
New Zealanders now took a hand in
smuggling British Imperial coinage,
exporting the silver pieces in cased

lots after 'sweeps' through the
country to gather such coinage in.
In 1933, therefore, the Government
announced immediate arrangements
for the provision of a local coinage.

The Coinage Committee, the
Coinage Designs Committee and all
others connected with the new
coinage, acted with commendable
speed, such that a well designed
New Zealand coinage actually began
to appear dated 1933. In
denominations it followed the
British model, a Crown being added
in 1935, partly in honour of the
Jubilee of King George V. A
commemorative Halfcrown was
struck in 1940 to celebrate the
centenary of the Treaty of Waitangi.
Bronze Pennies and Halfpennies
were added in 1940, but no
Farthings were ever needed. This
coinage, altered in design as
necessary over the reigns of George
V, George VI and Elizabeth II,
remained in use till decimalization
in 1967.

THE COIN REACHES THE MACHINE-1

174 *A German Rocker Press, dating from the seventeenth century.*

The beginnings of milled coinage seem to have been in Italy. Bramante (1444–1514), the celebrated architect who began the construction of St Peter's at Rome, appears to have been the first to use a screw press for striking Papal bulls, that is, the leaden seals appended to Papal edicts. Improved methods of medal making had been considered by Italian medallists. Previously medals had been cast, but the artists now sought a method by which a circular piece of metal could be obtained that was more perfect in shape and smoother and flatter than could be produced by a casting. Cristofano Caradosso, an Italian goldsmith, medallist and coin and gem engraver of the same period, is recorded as having used Bramante's press for striking some of his medals. Leonardo da Vinci (1452–1519) improved the press, devised another which would cut out circular blanks of metal, and made a light rolling mill through which metal could be passed to render it of reasonably even thickness. Benvenuto Cellini (1500–71), an artist celebrated for his fine medals, used all three types of machine, initially for producing medals and later for striking coins. Experiments were carried out with a drop press and the rolling mill was adapted in experiments to 'roll' the design on to coins instead of striking it.

These ideas seem to have spread to Germany, where there is a record of an Augsburg workman making a machine that would produce perfectly round flans with clear-cut edges, suitable for coins. Knowledge of this reached Henry II of France who, like all other rulers, was faced with the problem of forged hammered coins. It was claimed that by using the Augsburg machine, which produced pieces of regular shape, forgery became much more difficult, if not impossible. Henry bought the invention, and a German workman, Eric Hildegarde, helped the French Mint Master, Aubin Olivier, to install it in Paris between 1550 and 1553. The whole installation appears to have consisted of rolling mills, draw-benches and cutting and striking presses. By 1555 the Paris 'Monnaie du Moulin', so called because a mill (water?) was used as the motive power, was producing coins some of which even had raised letters on the rim, an added deterrent to the forger and one long used for this purpose.

News of these improvements soon reached London and a mill was set up at the Tower Mint in 1554. A certain amount of experimental work is said to have been undertaken and to have proved a failure.

Nothing more was done till 1561, when Eloi Mestrell, an employee of the Paris mint, fled to England. Here he was given premises in the Tower Mint and a salary of £25 a year and was allowed to install screw presses both for cutting blanks and for stamping coins. He does not appear to have put in any rolling mills. He met with opposition from his fellow employees, who feared his methods might cost them their employment. Coins continued to be struck in small quantity by Mestrell till 1572. In that year Richard Martin, in the course of evaluating Mestrell's machinery and methods of production, condemned them as being ten times as slow as the hand methods and turned Mestrell out of the Tower Mint. Mestrell is said to have been hanged in 1578 for counterfeiting.

A few machine-made coins began to appear during the reign of Charles I (1625–49). These were the work of Nicholas Briot, who had been Chief Engraver at the Paris mint from 1606 till 1625. Here his improved methods of coining did not meet with very much

MACHINA NOVA, quá, XVIII vel XX virorum auxilio circumactá, Nummi Svecorum metallici, vulgo Metall Plåtar, horæ ſpatio circiter 500 ſignantur. Auctore et Struct: M Lundſtröm A 1714.

176 *Swedish 'Plate Money' being marked by a man-driven hammerpress.*

encouragement and he went to England where he was appointed to a similar post in 1632.

Accounts of the types of machine which Briot used seem to vary. At the Tower Mint he appears to have made use of rolling mills to prepare the metal, cutting presses and screw-stamping presses. The accuracy and quality of his work are both excellent and he might have done more but for the Civil War. Briot was also for a time Master of the Scottish mint in Edinburgh–Scotland had a separate coinage of its own at this period–and here again he installed machines and struck some very fine coinage.

At the end of the Civil War the Commonwealth (1649–60) issued

hammered coinage from the Tower Mint, but experiments with modernization of the coining methods were started again. In Paris machine-made coins had started to be struck again in late 1639 in competition with hand-made coins. During a recoinage of French silver in 1641 the hand-made coinage methods again came under challenge, to lose the day. In 1645 French hammered coinage ceased.

The hammered coinage's very plain design which appeared from the Tower Mint in and after 1649 was struck from dies engraved by Thomas Simon who, after a period of joint-engravership, was appointed Chief Engraver in that year. He held the post till 1660, and died in the Great Plague of London in 1665. He was to see, and be ousted by, the great changes which were about to occur in English coinage.

Shadows of coming events began to fall in 1649, the first year of the Commonwealth government. After the success of the machine-made coins in France, Peter Blondeau was invited to go to England. He accepted at once, but was immediately met by vitriolic opposition from the workers at the Tower, such that it was not till May 1651 that he was able to use his machinery to produce coins. The uproar continued, however, the Mint workers declaring that they could produce better coins than Blondeau on some old machines—probably Briot's—that were lying around the Mint. Taking them at their word, a trial of skill was ordered between Blondeau, using his machinery, and David Ramage the provost of the moneyers, who was to use the old machines referred to. Simon supplied the dies for Blondeau's coins which, in fairness, were better struck than those produced by Ramage. The result of the competition seems to have been inconclusive, since Blondeau appears to have been given permission to continue striking.

It was now decided, on the order of Oliver Cromwell and with the consent of the Council, to strike a coinage having Cromwell's head on the obverse, like any king, and his arms on the reverse. Blondeau was given the work and provided with separate premises in Drury House, at a safe distance from the 'protesters' at the Tower. A Spanish treasure which had been captured in 1656 was brought to the Mint for coining into money. Blondeau obtained a small portion and between 1656 and 1658 produced a series of gold and silver milled coins with the use of his machinery. Once again the dies were made by Thomas Simon and a very finely executed coinage resulted. Cromwell promised Blondeau a further £1,400 worth of new machinery—a considerable sum in the seventeenth century—and all seemed to be going well for the Frenchman, even though the Tower was still producing large quantities of hammered coinage.

Such important changes as those envisaged in abandoning hammered

177   Obverse of a Charles II Sixpence struck by the mill and screw press.

178   Pistrucci's original reverse for the milled Sovereign, used only in 1817, 1818 and 1820. The Garter was then removed, the St George motif enlarged, and in this form the design is still used on Sovereigns of the present reign.

179 a, b   The reverse of the Charles II Halfcrown with one of the five obverses (179 b).

coinage, against long accepted practice and strong prejudice against the change, are not usually made overnight. But for the death of Cromwell in 1658 milled coinage might well have been gradually accepted. In the event Blondeau's coinage was never officially used, though examples appear from time to time with all the appearance of having been in circulation. The death of Cromwell and the loss of his support made it politic for Blondeau to go back to France, soon to return, however. Meanwhile Charles II was recalled from exile on the Continent and proclaimed King on 5 May 1660; he returned to England on 29 May. In August 1660 the Tower Mint appears to have had a clear-out, probably in preparation for the coinage of the new reign, and Blondeau's machinery, together with that of Briot and Mestrell, was shipped to Edinburgh.

This disposal of machinery seems to have been somewhat premature, though it was to react to the benefit of Blondeau. For the first two years of his reign Charles II adopted his father's types of hammered coinage, the dies being made once more by Thomas Simon. Clipping and counterfeiting appear to have been so serious that the King in Council ordered that all coins should be struck by machinery, with grained or lettered edges, as soon as possible. In April 1662 Blondeau was again invited to England and by agreement provided all the necessary machinery for striking coinage by the mill and screw press. One great point in the agreement was that he was to take with him his 'secret' process for marking the edges of coins with lettering or graining. Great faith was put in this method of marking the coins, since it would make it virtually impossible for coins to be clipped—a plain-edged coin would at once arouse suspicion—and if the edge-marking process was kept secret, counterfeiters would be overcome. Indeed, so secret was it kept that as late as the nineteenth century certain mint operatives had to take oath not to disclose how the edges of coins were marked, though the process had long since become common knowledge and advanced considerably since Blondeau's time.

The question now arose as to who should design the new coinage. The old complex of gold denominations—

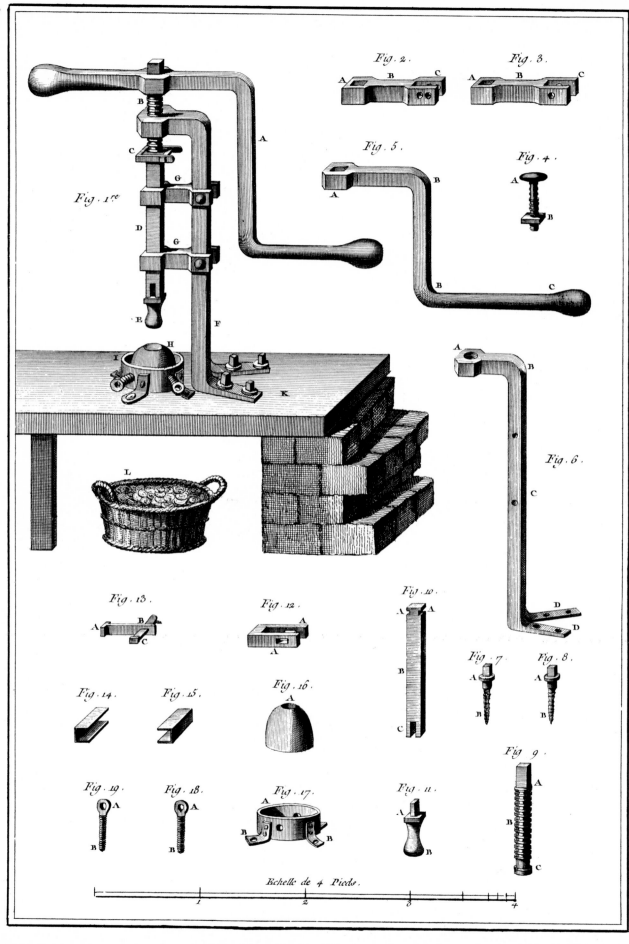

Fig. 2.   Fig. 3.

Fig. 5.   Fig. 4.

Fig. 1re

Fig. 6.

Fig. 13.   Fig. 12.   Fig. 10.

Fig. 14.   Fig. 15.   Fig. 16.   Fig. 7.   Fig. 8.

Fig. 9.

Fig. 19.   Fig. 18.   Fig. 17.   Fig. 11.

Echelle de 4 Pieds.

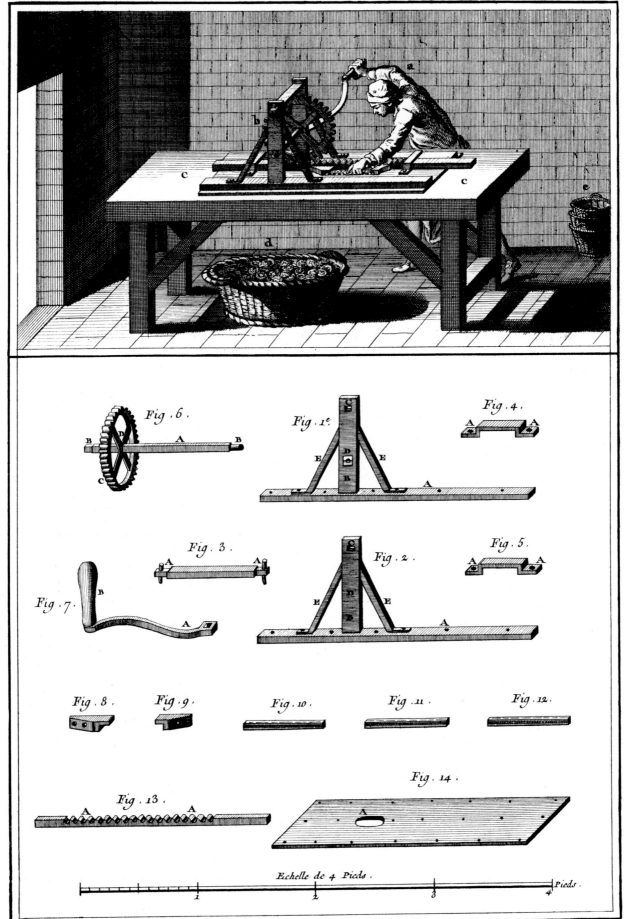

Fig. 6.

Fig. 1ᵉ.

Fig. 4.

Fig. 3.

Fig. 2.

Fig. 5.

Fig. 7.

Fig. 8. Fig. 9. Fig. 10. Fig. 11. Fig. 12.

Fig. 14.

Fig. 13.

Echelle de 4 Pieds.

Pieds.

1 2 3 4

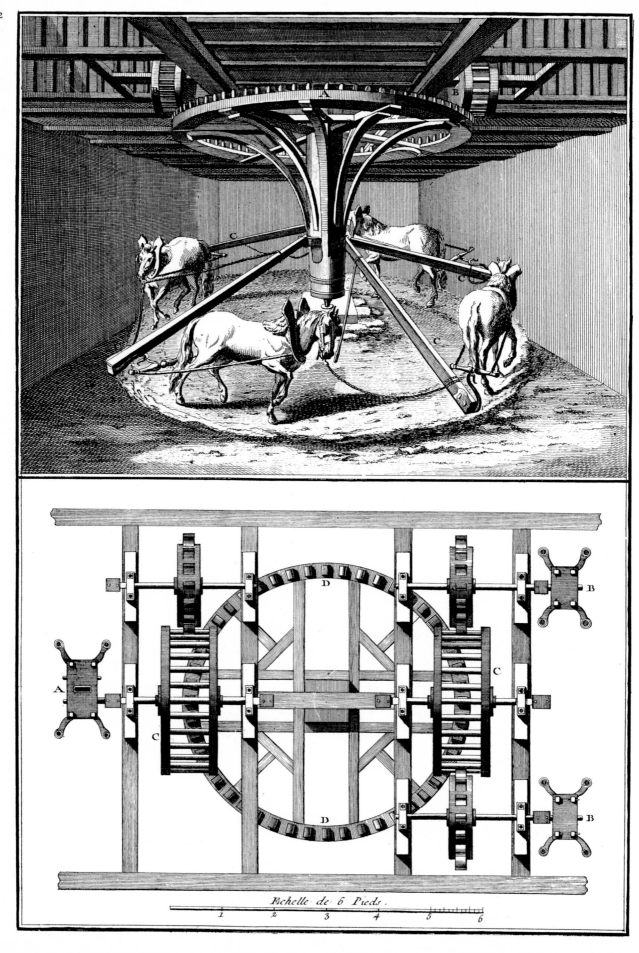

Echelle de 6 Pieds.

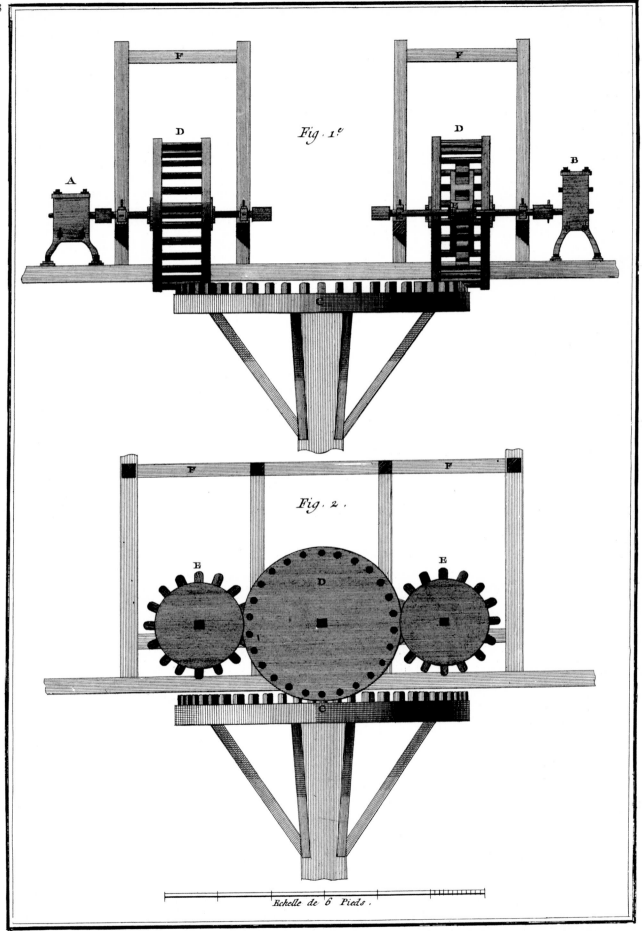

Fig. 1.ᵉ

Fig. 2.

Echelle de 6 Pieds.

180, 181 *French prints, dated c. 1755, of early machines and their component parts: a Blank Cutter (180) and Edge Marking (181).*

182, 183 *A Rolling Mill driven by horses, together with diagrams explaining the intricacies of the machinery.*

184, 185 *Press and dies used in the Mint during the reign of George II.*

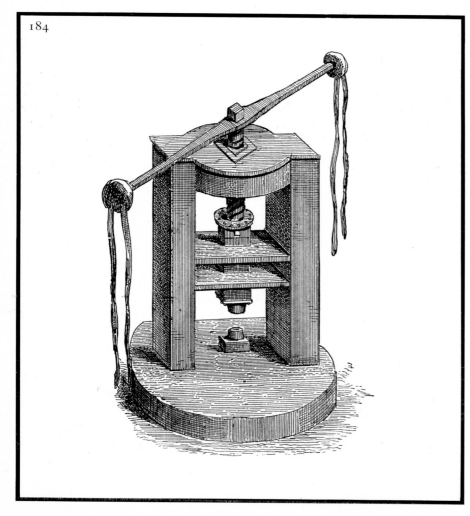

184

Broads, Unites, Double-crowns, Crowns and the like—were to be replaced with four simple denominations. Of these the Guinea was the unit, with multiples of £5 5s 0d, £2 2s 0d and a Half-guinea. Silver denominations, from Crown to Penny, were to remain the same.

By right of tenure of office Thomas Simon should have engraved the new coinage, but there were underground political—or rather Royalist—forces at work. While in exile in the Low Countries Charles had become acquainted with the Roettier family. The father, Philip Roettier (the name is sometimes spelt Roettiers or Rotier), was a goldsmith and medallist at Antwerp. He is said to have lent Charles money and in return the exiled King had promised that, should he return to the throne of England, places for Philip's three sons, John, Joseph and Philip, should be found at the Tower Mint.

True to his word, Charles II invited John and Joseph, shortly to be followed by Philip, to England in 1661 to work at the Tower Mint. Early in 1662 John Roettier and Thomas Simon were ordered to engrave the dies for the new coinage, in gold and silver, but 'by reason of a contest in Art between them, we (the Mint Board) do at present find it very difficult to bring them to any agreement'. Blondeau received a twenty-one-year contract for maintenance of the new machinery and tools, apart from those in the melting house and gravers' shop, and for instructing the moneyers. He also was paid piece-work rates for the use of his 'secret' process of rounding and lettering the coin edges.

This contract virtually spelled Simon's defeat. It had been concluded in April 1662, and by 19 May all three Roettier brothers had been formally appointed engravers at the Tower while Simon was relegated to the engraving of dies for medals and seals. Simon, however, was to go down fighting. In 1663 he produced his celebrated 'Petition Crown'. The beautifully designed and executed piece was his last attempt to convince the King and the Council that his work was superior to that of Roettier. To emphasize this, the coin contained on its edge a legend, in two lines, which read: THOMAS SIMON MOST HVMBLY

PRAYS YOVR MAJESTY TO COMPARE THIS HIS TRYALL PIECE WITH THE DVTCH AND IF MORE TRVLY DRAWN & EMBOSS'D MORE GRACE FVLLY ORDER'D AND MORE ACCVRATELY ENGRAVEN TO RELEIVE (sic) HIM. To imprint a legend of such a length in a double line, with some of the lettering in fine script, round the thickness of the coin, was in itself a remarkable achievement—and would be so even now. Presumably since Blondeau held the edge-marking 'secret' he accomplished the actual edge-marking himself.

Of this extremely rare pattern for a Crown only fifteen are now known. Simon produced another, the edge of which read REDDITE QVAE CAESARIS CAESARI &CT POST followed by the sun rising from behind clouds, meaning 'Render unto Caesar the things which are Caesar's etc. the sun shines after the storm'. Nine of these rare patterns are known. The sun did not shine on Simon again. Three years later he was dead, a victim of the last and worst plague of London.

Something should now be said about the actual machines used to strike the new coinage of Charles II. The term 'milled coinage' comes in fact from the source of power used to drive the rollers which reduced the metal to an even thickness. The 'milling' on the edge of modern coins is more properly termed graining. It has to be remembered that the coins of Charles II, and of many monarchs who were to succeed him, were marked either with the legend DECVS ET TVTAMEN—an ornament and a safeguard (against clipping)—and the regnal year ANNO REGNI XV, the fifteenth year of our reign; or with knurling, a screw-thread type of graining.

The source of power installed at the Tower in 1662 when Blondeau provided the new machinery took the form of a horse mill, which consisted of a basement chamber, between the floor and roof of which a large vertical capstan was fitted. Four horses, attached to capstan bars, trod an endless journey round and round, causing the capstan to revolve. Two horses were kept as relief workers for each mill, two of which were installed. The top of the capstan had a large gear-wheel,

several feet in diameter and with vertical teeth attached to it—a type of gear which has now developed into the crown-wheel. The teeth of this gear were probably made of boxwood. Placed east and west, at ceiling level, were two squirrel-cage pinions, engaging with the crown-wheel, and from these shafts drove the rolling mill on the floor above.

The rolling mill was very like a domestic mangle, with wrought, later cast, iron rollers, four inches in diameter. The maker of the rollers ensured for himself a nice little income by refusing to sell them to the Mint, but hiring them at ten shillings a day. Three passages through the rollers were, at that time, sufficient to reduce the metal to a strip of the required thickness, the strip being called a fillet.

The fillet next went to the blank cutter. This was quite a simple machine, consisting of a vertical shaft with the cutter on the bottom, the shaft being forced down by a weighted lever fixed horizontally across the top to a screw-threaded vertical rod. The blanks were then cut out as one would cut dough from a strip of pastry; the scissel— that is, the metal left over when the blanks had been cut—was sent back for remelting and rolling.

Next came the famous edge-marking machine. While Blondeau was alive the blanks were passed to him for the process. In fact his 'secret' machine was really quite simple. It consisted of two horizontal parallel bars on one or both of which the legend (or part of the legend) or, as the case may be, the graining, was engraved. One bar was secured to a table, the other was caused to slide parallel to the first through a gear, which engaged with teeth on the bar, and which was turned by a crank handle. Springs exerted the necessary pressure and kept the bars tight against the blank. The blank was placed between the bars, the handle turned, the movable bar caused the blank to revolve, at the same time imprinting the lettering or graining on the edge of the blank. Nothing could be simpler—or slower. It is fairly obvious that Blondeau, who insisted on marking each and every coin edge himself, was the bottle-neck. Every coin to be struck had to pass through his hands, and one-at-a-time through his 'secret' machine which, however, he was

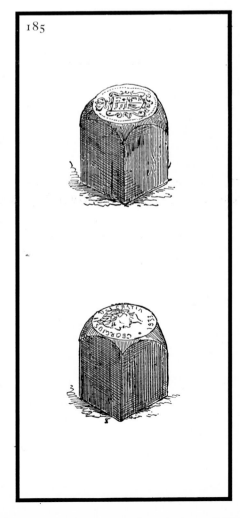

185

186 a

186 b

187

186 a, b *Obverse of the silver Crown of William and Mary, the only reign in which two busts appeared on the obverse of an English milled coin. (186 b) Reverse of the same coin. Note the odd position of the date, the 2 of which has been recut over an inverted 2.*

187 *Reverse of William and Mary Five Guinea piece.*

quite prepared to show to King Charles. The machine was, naturally, improved progressively, even in Blondeau's time, finally resulting in a collar of spring steel being used, the collar being in sections and marked with the necessary lettering or graining.

The edged blanks, having been annealed, blanched with alum and water and dried in sawdust, were then passed to the coining press. This, like the blank cutter, was a screw-operated capstan, the reverse die being on the lower end of the descending shaft. The obverse die was placed in position below the shaft on the bedplate at about floor level. The vertical shaft had two arms, the capstan 'bars', joined to it horizontally at the top end. Each arm carried a weight at the tip of 300 lb. of lead. Two ropes were fitted to each arm. Two men, or in the case of large coins like the Crown, four men, grasped the ropes and, hauling down on them, brought the upper die down on to the blank and forced the blank down on to the lower, obverse die, thus marking the coin and finishing its striking. A moneyer, sitting in a shallow pit in the floor in front of the press, flicked the struck coin away with his finger and inserted another blank while the press was being wound up for another blow. At top speed these presses could produce a coin every two seconds, though the average rate seems to have been about twenty-six coins per minute, with three men working the press.

The metals, gold and silver—copper was still being experimente with, not very successfully—had, o course, to be melted, refined, alloyed, assayed and so forth before they went through these processes to turn them into coins. These quite simple machines were something of a nine days' wonder in 1662. They continued to develop, to be improved upon and new and better machines were invented as time went on. Basically, however, coins in England, and for the whole of Britain after the Act of Union with Scotland in the reign of Queen Anne (1702–14) when the Scottish mint was abolished, continued to be produced by this method until the next great coinage reform at the beginning of the nineteenth century.

The various coins which were so produced from 1662 till 1813 contain much of interest. It was

stated earlier that the gold issues were simplified and the silver remained the same. For the sake of clarity they are listed:

Gold £5 5s, £2 2s, £1 1s and 10s 6d (Half-guinea).

Silver Crown (5s), Halfcrown (2s 6d), Shilling, Sixpence, Fourpence (Groat), Threepence, Twopence (Half-groat), Penny.

Copper (Halfpennies and Farthings were struck during the period, never in quantity and with various technical difficulties. Some of each denomination were also for a brief period struck in tin.)

The gold unit was the Guinea. It obtained its name from the fact that much of the metal from which it was struck came from Guinea in Africa and the Gold Coast in general. Some of it was supplied by the Africa Company, part of whose arms, an elephant, sometimes with a castle-like howdah on its back, appears from time to time below the bust of the monarch. The upper multiples, the Five- and Two-guineas, were not, it is thought, much used in general circulation. They were the 'bullion' with which the financiers of the day carried out large transactions. Throughout the period Five-guineas and even Two-guineas were large sums of money to the average person.

The designs were simple. The monarch's head occupied the obverse, and four crowned shields of arms, of England, Scotland, France and Ireland, the reverse; with four sceptres in saltire in the angles. In the reign of William and Mary (1689–94) the head of both King and Queen appeared on the obverse since they reigned as joint monarchs. The coins of this reign are the only ones in the milled series to have two heads on the obverse side. The four shields of arms on the reverse gave place to one large crowned shield, and though the four shields returned in the reigns of William III (1694–1702), Anne (1702–14) and George I (1714–27), the single crowned shield was used again in the reign of George II (1727–60). It was also used in the first part of the reign of George III (1760–1820), though only Guineas and Half-guineas were struck.

Mint or initial marks in the form seen on hammered coins were no longer used on milled coinage. Sources of metal were, however,

KING · W · QUEEM

188   *William and Mary Delftware
dish. William was, of course, Prince of
Orange before succeeding to the
English and Scottish thrones.*

frequently indicated. The elephant and elephant and castle have already been mentioned. On some of the gold coins (as well as silver) of Queen Anne the word VIGO appears below the bust. This indicates that the metal was captured at the naval battle of Vigo Bay, where the combined British and Dutch fleets captured or sank a merchant fleet of French and Spanish vessels. Though hailed as a great naval victory, it now appears that the action was more of an economic disaster.

On some of the gold and silver coins of George II the word LIMA appears below the bust. This is now said to indicate metal captured by Admiral Anson from the Spanish in the Philippines on his round-the-world voyage, with the addition of other metal captured from the same source by a number of freebooters in the Atlantic.

While there are varieties of busts on the Five- and Two-guinea pieces in any one reign, the reverse usually remained the same. On the Guineas and Half-guineas, these being struck in greater quantities than the larger pieces, not only are there often several bust varieties for any one monarch—usually altered as he or she grew older—but also in the reigns of George I and George II there are many reverse types. In the latter reign the so-called 'Spade' Guinea, thus named on account of the shape of the shield on the reverse, is by far the best known. It was popularized by fiction writers and, after the end of the Guinea as a denomination, frequently worn as a watch-chain ornament by Victorian gentlemen. It was also copied in brass as a playing counter.

One has come to look upon the Guinea as 21s in value. This was not always the case. At various times between 1662 and 1813 its value has fluctuated. One reason for fixing the Pound value of the Sovereign at the coinage reform of 1816 was that the Guinea had reached a value at which it was difficult to calculate—something like 27s.

For a brief period of one year, 1718, during the reign of George I, little gold Quarter-guineas—Guineas in miniature—were struck. This denomination was struck again in 1762 (George III), as were Third-guineas from 1797 till 1813. These were brief issues, and apart from them the gold coinage remained as listed above.

189 a, b *George I Shilling (looped tie variety) with the Roses and Plumes reverse.*

190 a, b *George III Halfcrown, with the laureate head of more normal dimensions than the earlier 'bull' issue. Nevertheless the King still looks like some epicene leftover from decadent Rome.*

191 a, b *Anne gold Five Guineas. The obverse has VIGO below the bust denoting gold captured there from the Spaniards in 1702; the reverse is Pre-Union, with a rose in the centre as opposed to the Post-Union gold coins which have the Star of the Most Noble Order of the Garter. The silver denominations all have this Star, except the Maundy money.*

189 a

190 a

189 b

190 b

It can scarcely be alleged that Roettier had a particularly difficult piece of work in providing designs for the new coinage. The first of all the new coins to be struck was the Crown in 1662. The design was slightly amended and when production proper got under way in 1663 it will be seen that the silver coins down to the Sixpence were almost exactly the same as the gold, minus the sceptres in the angles, which had been replaced with two interlinked Cs. The Star of the Most Noble Order of the Garter usually formed the centre piece between the four crowned shields. Save for the reign of William and Mary this type of design remained in use for all the silver pieces, even those of George II and the first part of George III's reign. After the death of Charles II the Cs in the angles naturally disappeared.

In the reign of William III it was decided to call in the last of the hammered coinage still in circulation and replace it with milled coinage. This caused a panic at the Mint, since there was more work than it could cope with. Branch mints were set up in Bristol, Chester, Exeter, Norwich and York. These all struck silver coins only, apart from the Crown, and these coins carried the initial letter of the mint at which they were struck below the bust in the years 1696 and 1697.

Sources of metal indicators appeared on the silver coins as follows:
Rose—metal from west of England mines.
Elephant, or Elephant and Castle—the Africa Company.
Plume—Welsh mines.
Roses and Plumes—the new 'Company for smelting down lead'.
VIGO—as for gold.
SSC—supplied by the South Seas Company after its bankruptcy.
LIMA—as for gold.
WCC—Welsh Copper Company.

With both gold and silver pieces, after the union with Scotland in the reign of Anne, the arms of Scotland were halved with those of England. When George I succeeded to the throne the arms of the Electorate were added on one of the four shields. The arms of France, to which Britain had no claim since the reign of Philip and Mary, continued to be shown till the recoinage in the second part of the reign of George III: the French titles were dropped from the legend at the same time.

191 b

191 a

192 *Coining Presses in the Tower Mint, early nineteenth century.*

193 a, b *Simon's celebrated 'Petition Crown' of 1663, a beautifully designed piece aimed at convincing Charles II that his work was superior to Roettier's. Unfortunately his effort was in vain.*

193 a

193 b

THE COIN REACHES THE MACHINE-2

During the latter part of the eighteenth century the coinage in Britain had reached a very low ebb. No Five- or Two-guinea pieces had been struck during the reign of George III (1760–1820), but Guineas and Half-guineas were struck till 1813. With the silver coinage matters became serious. From 1760 till 1787 the only pieces to be issued were Shillings in 1763 and Maundy money. In 1787 large quantities of Shillings and Sixpences were struck but many of these must have been kept as souvenirs as they frequently appear today in almost mint state. In 1797 the Bank of England resorted to the extraordinary expedient of issuing Spanish Dollars and their subdivisions stamped with the head of George III in an oval indent. In 1804 this stamp was changed for a similar head in an octagonal indent.

Both pieces were extensively forged, there being plenty of Spanish Dollars available on the bullion market. The countermarked pieces were put into circulation at 4s 9d, giving rise to the description 'two kings' heads and not worth a crown', since both the Spanish and the English kings' heads now appeared on them.

To counter the forgers the Bank received permission to issue Bank of England Dollars between 1804 and 1815, though they were all dated 1804. Smaller denominations designated 'Bank Tokens' were dated till 1816. The larger pieces were made from Spanish Dollars which the Bank sent to Boulton and Watt's mint in Birmingham (of which more later) to have the original design planed off and restamped. As a result it is sometimes possible to see on these pieces faint traces of the original Spanish design and lettering below that of the new.

Part of the reason for all these extraordinary events was that the war which followed the French Revolution was soon putting a heavy strain on the country's finances. Gold and silver fluctuated in value and the relationship between British coinage and the coinages of the European countries was in an unsatisfactory state. The whole matter was constantly under review and a Committee on Coin was eventually set up to attempt to deal with it. After a great deal of argument and controversy about metal values, the intrinsic value of gold and silver coins, bimetallic currency and so on, which lasted from the late eighteenth century till 1816, a new coinage was decided upon and an Act passed to that effect on 22 June. This resulted in the Sovereign and Half-sovereign, the former still being struck though not now circulating in Britain, and the range of silver coins from 5s to Maundy Penny–for practical purposes from 5s to 6d. The silver coins, though changed to cupro-nickel in 1947, remained in use till decimalization, with denominations like the Halfcrown disappearing with the approach of decimalization.

The Committee on Coin had another serious matter to deal with. The Royal Mint had been located in the Tower of London for some five hundred years. During this time it had gradually extended its buildings in a half-circle within the ramparts from the river in the west back to the river in the east. This elongated series of buildings must have been completely uneconomical and most inconvenient to manage, with various processes in different places, resulting in much waste of time and effort.

At the same time the Tower was in use as a fortress, the army occupying the remainder. They now began to put increasing pressure on the Mint to relinquish more space, which they needed for the wounded coming back from the French Wars.

The Committee on Coin examined both this situation and the actual equipment of the Mint itself. As has been said previously, the machinery in use was basically much the same as that installed in 1662 – certainly production methods had varied little though there had been improvements in the 150-year interval. Meanwhile, in the eighteenth century, events had been taking place in Birmingham which were to affect the whole future of the Royal Mint, the method of striking coins and their actual appearance. These events were brought about by Matthew Boulton and James Watt.

Matthew Boulton, FRS, was a Birmingham manufacturer of fancy articles in silver, steel and brass. He inherited the business in 1759 and in 1762 built the Soho Manufactory, using the dammed Hockley Brook as a source of water power. In 1767 he extended the Manufactory and was patronized by George III, who took an interest in his productions. He first met James Watt, the taciturn Scots engineer who improved the steam engine, in 1768 and in 1774 acquired Dr Roebuck's interest in Watt's steam engine patent and persuaded Watt to come to Birmingham. In 1775 Watt's patent was extended for twenty-five years and he entered into partnership with Boulton.

One of the outcomes of the partnership was the supply of steam engines for such purposes as pumping at the Cornish tin mines and at coal mines, and in 1786 Boulton applied steam power to coining. He improved both the coining press and the method of coin manufacture and was soon executing a coinage for the East India Company. He also supplied his steam coining machinery to the Moscow mint.

At the time when the Committee on Coin was considering the whole matter of coinage, Boulton appeared before the Privy Council on the question. His main object was the establishment of a proper coinage in base metal, such as copper, to satisfy the great need for small change and to counter the large amount of forged Halfpence and Farthings which had come into being due to the shortage of any adequate form of small money. In 1790 he took out a patent for his improved coining press and in 1797 was given a contract to produce a copper

coinage for Britain. In 1799 he received a further contract for, and began to fit up, his coining machinery in the Royal Mint.

As previously stated, the Committee on Coin considered the location and equipment of the Royal Mint itself in their general deliberations. They called in John Rennie, F.R.S., in 1798 to examine the Mint machinery and produce a report. (Rennie is perhaps better known as the designer of the first Waterloo Bridge, Southwark Bridge and the London Bridge which is being replaced as these words are written.) Rennie's Report of 10 July 1798 found little that was right with the Mint, its methods of coin production and its machinery. Conversion to steam power, with the new machinery that went with it, was the main recommendation, together with the inevitable revolution in minting methods which would go with such modernization.

After consideration the Committee on Coin voted in favour of steam power. In August 1804 they asked Rennie to find out from the Tower authorities if the installation of steam power at the Mint would endanger the fortress. The authorities would have none of it. If the Mint intended to set itself on fire or blow itself up with steam power it should not be allowed to do so in the Tower. They had been gradually encroaching on the Mint premises within the walls; they now demanded the whole, pleading the necessities of war. It was therefore agreed that the Mint should leave the Tower, and be set up in its own establishment on a site across the road on Little Tower Hill. Contracts were signed in November 1805, with Rennie for the buildings and with Boulton for the machinery. The architect for the new buildings was James Johnson, who died in 1807, Sir Robert Smirke being appointed to continue the work to Johnson's designs. The building which arose, with its fine courtyard and twin gatehouses, is that which is now seen from the northern approach to the Tower Bridge. The remainder of the buildings are later additions. (Though the Royal Mint is once more on the move, this time to South Wales, it is expected that this original building will remain.) The new building was finished in 1809. The Mint moved in by

195 *Medal of William Wellesley-Pole, elder brother of the Duke of Wellington and Master Worker at the Mint from 1812.*

196 a, b *Silver crown of 1818, designed by Pistrucci, Wellesley-Pole's protégé and a controversial figure at the Mint. The obverse is a caricature of George III, and the artist insisted on signing his name in full on both sides of the coin. This was greeted with a deal of sarcastic comment.*

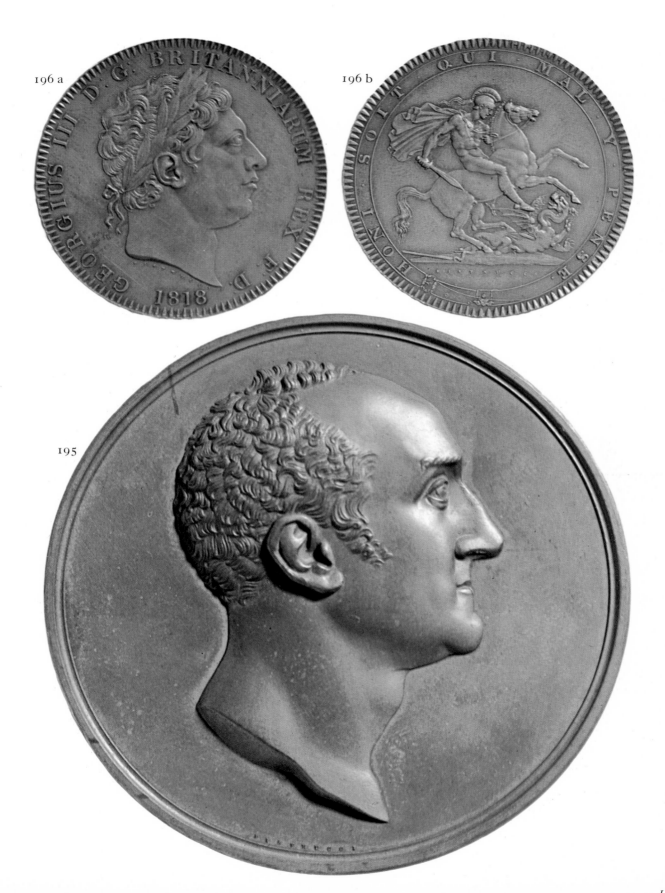

196 a

196 b

195

stages and in August 1812 finally handed over its premises to the Constable of the Tower. The Royal Mint was now an independent establishment.

The new and improved machinery supplied by Boulton and Watt is of interest. The main sources of power were four rotative steam engines, which drew their supply of water through a tunnel from the Tower moat, which in those days was filled. The first engine of thirty horsepower drove three rolling mills, each of a different capacity, which broke down the ingots of gold and silver into fillets ready for blank cutting.

There were twelve presses for blank cutting, driven by a sixteen-horsepower engine. The presses were arranged in a circle below a large horizontal wheel. This, revolving sixty-four times a minute, drove the punches down in succession by the action of what would now be called cams. The punches were of at least three sizes to provide the blanks for the various denominations.

Eight coining presses were installed. These were driven by a ten-horsepower engine, again through an overhead horizontal wheel. The action of the wheel was to draw up the pistons of two air-tight cylinders attached to each press. When released the pistons descended sharply by the vacuum power they had created on the rising stroke. On this recoil stroke a heavily loaded bar was spun round by pivots and this drove a spiral column downwards on to the blank. The reverse die was attached to the descending column and the obverse die was in the bedplate below the blank, and at each stroke—sixty a minute—a coin was struck. An automatic device was incorporated which placed the blank in the correct position and a collar which rose up to hold the blank and imprint the graining on the coin's edge. A counting device was also incorporated.

Finally a six-horsepower steam engine was a maid-of-all-work, driving new die-cutting lathes and a number of milling, shaking and pulverizing machines. Three screw presses of the old type were still used for making punches, dies and medals, and were still actuated by manpower, six men to a press. These continued in use till 1899.

Into this brand new Mint, with its magnificent new buildings and its 'stupendous and beautiful' new machinery, stepped William Wellesley-Pole in 1812, with the title of Master Worker. He was elder brother of Arthur Wellesley, Duke of Wellington, and he became Wellesley-Pole in acknowledgment of a legacy. In modern parlance he would be classified as an experienced technocrat. On his shoulders fell not only the major reorganization of the Mint, in which rising salaries and reduced expenditure were the order of the day—as well as the getting rid of a number of ancient 'customs', some not above reproach —but also the superintendence of the launching of the new coinage. In this field he made one slip, which was to cost him, his successors and finally the Treasury, reams of paper and spilled ink and quite a lot of money.

The Committee on Coin had arranged in 1811 the transfer of the two Thomas Wyons, father and son, from Boulton's mint in Birmingham to the Royal Mint in London. They and their collaterals and descendants were to be, as it happened, the main Mint engravers for over eighty years.

At this point the Italian artist and gem engraver, Benedetto Pistrucci, a refugee from France after the fall of Napoleon in 1814, arrived in London, via Rome. As a gem engraver and maker of cameos his work was of the finest quality. He soon became patronized in Britain, and Sir Joseph Banks paid him fifty Guineas for making a portrait of George III as a jasper cameo. In 1816 Banks introduced Pistrucci to the Master of the Mint, Wellesley-Pole, who gave the jasper cameo of George III to Thomas Wyon junior, the then Chief Engraver to the Royal Mint, to be copied for the obverse of the Halfcrown of the new coinage. Thomas Wyon's copy of the work of another artist was not considered satisfactory and was disapproved. This is not unexpected. The copying by one artist of the work of another is always liable to produce something less fine than the original work; and it must be remembered that, while Wyon was a highly skilled engraver of coin dies, Pistrucci was a gem and cameo cutter, with no knowledge of the requirements of cutting dies for the reproduction of coinage.

198

Pistrucci suggested that St George and the dragon was a suitable reverse design for the new gold coinage. Wellesley-Pole commissioned him to make a cameo of the design in jasper, for which he paid the artist one hundred Guineas. At this point Thomas Wyon died (1817) and Wellesley-Pole, having in mind the unsuccessful attempt to copy Pistrucci's portrait of George III, felt that it was necessary to employ Pistrucci himself to engrave both the head of George III and the St George reverse on the dies for the new coinage.

This is where the point of controversy arose. Pistrucci always maintained that Wellesley-Pole offered him the post of Chief Engraver at the Royal Mint so that he could execute the necessary work for the new coinage. Wellesley-Pole contended that he had not made such an offer. The dispute continued over many years after Wellesley-Pole had left the Mint, and it finally took Gladstone himself to settle the matter.

It should be said that, even if Wellesley-Pole had offered the position of Chief Engraver to Pistrucci, he (Wellesley-Pole) could not in fact have given the artist this appointment. Under an Act passed during the reign of William III

(1694–1702), it had been decided that a foreigner could not be appointed to this position. In the event, when Wellesley-Pole found he could not appoint Pistrucci, the post of Chief Engraver was left vacant and Pistrucci was granted an official residence within the Mint, with the necessary working facilities and a salary of £500 a year, and given the work of designing the new coinage. This arrangement was never put into writing, and for the rest of his life Pistrucci contended that he had been offered the official position, which he never obtained.

The range of coins now set up under the reform of 1816 did not alter the coinage structure very greatly. Only the methods of production and the accuracy of the finished product by shape and weight were improved. The range of coins now was:

Gold Sovereign and Half-sovereign.
Silver Crown, Halfcrown, Shilling,
   Sixpence and Fourpence to Penny
   struck for Maundy money, but
   technically legal tender.

There were also some copper coins, about which more will be said later.

It will be seen that the main change simply substituted the

197, 198 *Matthew Boulton, and his Manufactory at Soho near Birmingham where he produced his steam-powered coining machinery.*

199 *John Rennie, who recommended that the Mint be modernized and converted to steam power.*

200 a, b   *In keeping with the Gothic revival in Victorian England, a Gothic Florin and a Gothic Crown were struck, apparently on the suggestion of the Queen. This gold proof Crown, dated 1847, could certainly be counted one of the handsomest to have been produced in Britain.*

201   *The reverse of a 1797 2d piece, one of a series of large thick coins that came to be known as 'Cartwheels'.*

200 a

201

200 b

Sovereign and Half-sovereign for the Guinea and Half-guinea. Apparently provision was made for the striking of £5 and £2 pieces to replace the £5 5s and £2 2s, probably as the occasion should require. In actual fact, though these pieces did appear over the next 150 years, sometimes only as proof coins, it is very doubtful if the non-proof pieces ever actually entered circulation.

The Sovereign and the Crown carried Pistrucci's designs, a caricature of George III on the obverse and the St George and the dragon in all its magnificence on the reverse. This reverse design soon became a tradition and still appears on the 1968 Sovereign. It appeared at its best on the Crowns of 1818–20. Here it was enclosed within the Garter of the Most Noble Order of the Garter, a most suitable frame for such a subject. The artist decided to sign his name in full, PISTRUCCI, below the truncation of the neck of George III and below the groundline on the reverse. With the Wyon family working at the Mint and doing, as we shall see, magnificent work, Wellesley-Pole's protégé was unwelcome to many, including some of the more

prominent numismatists of the day. Acid comment was poured on the Italian, who insisted on signing his name in full, while the British artists hid behind tiny initials, such as T.W. or W.W.

Nor were things going particularly happily within the Mint. On instructions from 'above' some of Pistrucci's designs were 'touched up' by the Wyons, leading the Italian to complain that they had been spoiled. In actual fact so far as the coinage is concerned Pistrucci failed to produce a really pleasing design. His head of George III on the Halfcrowns of 1816–17 made the poor sick King look like an example of a Roman Emperor of the worst type. The pleasing reverse was designed by Thomas Wyon junior. The first type of obverse for the George III Halfcrowns soon earned the name 'bull head' for the effigy, and it was rapidly discarded. In 1817 a new head appeared on the Halfcrown but even this was not very flattering. Wyon's design for the reverse, similar to that for the first type, was modified by Pistrucci, not to its advantage. What had been a pleasing, if fussy, design now became strident. There was bad blood between Pistrucci and Wyon,

202, 203, 204 *The exterior of the Mint (202) on Little Tower Hill, designed by Johnson and completed by Smirke. The interior views show the Rolling Rooms (203) and the machines for cutting out Blanks (204). Both pictures are dated 1883.*

as well there might be. No artist likes to have his work altered by others. However, thanks to Wellesley-Pole's liking for Pistrucci's St George, the Mint was now 'stuck' with the Italian, who ceaselessly complained that he had been offered the post of Chief Engraver.

Pistrucci's 'Waterloo', in this the age of Waterloo, came about in the next reign. He designed the coinage for George IV (1820–30) and again produced a caricature of the King. Whatever may be said about George IV, he had an appreciation for art. He endured Pistrucci's caricature from his accession till 1823. He then commanded that, in future, his appearance on the coinage should follow that of a bust of him carved by Sir Francis Chantrey. Pistrucci was ordered to copy this bust for a new coinage. The Italian refused. He would not bend to copy the work of another whom, as an Englishman, he probably despised. This was Pistrucci's 'Waterloo' so far as Britain's coinage is concerned.

Much could still be told about how he hung on at the Mint, and was given a created appointment as Chief Medallist; how he cheated over the pupils this appointment allowed him, and how he held on to his post as the artist for George IV's magnificent Waterloo Medal. This was so large that it was never struck but was an artistic achievement worthy of the man who had produced the St George and the dragon for the Sovereign and Crown of George III. In the event, had the medal been struck as envisaged by George IV, by the time Pistrucci had completed the design there would have been no one left, out of all the victors of Waterloo, to receive it but the aged Iron Duke. This famous commemorative medal, the largest medal never struck, is another story and outside this work.

The coinage of George IV was the same as that of George III, save that a Two Pound piece was struck in 1823 and, from the very worn specimens that come into the hands of collectors, appears to have circulated. It was the last time a gold coin of this value seems to have been used as money.

The short reign of William IV (1830–7) saw nothing very spectacular in coinage design. The whole series from the Sovereign was engraved by W. Wyon, after a

203

204

portrait by Chantrey, with Merlen, assistant-engraver under Wyon, designing and engraving most of the reverses. St George and the dragon and indeed all trace of Pistrucci disappeared. No Crown piece was struck for circulation but a few proof pieces were made. The reverse contained a very detailed and heavily mantled shield of arms. Proof Two Pound pieces were struck in small numbers but none for circulation. In 1834 the size of the Half-sovereign was reduced but it returned to its original size the next year. An additional Fourpenny piece, the so-called 'Britannia Groat', was added to the series, at the instance of Sir Joseph Hume. It quickly became known as a 'Joey'.

These main denominations continued into the reign of Victoria (1837–1901), the Wyon family, William and Leonard Charles, being firmly established in the designing and engraving department. Pistrucci's St George was revived from time to time and de Saulles engraved most of the reverses for the last coinage of the reign.

There were in fact three main coinage types, known respectively as the 'Young head', 'Jubilee head' and 'Old head' series. The obverse of the Jubilee coinage was designed by Sir Joseph Boehm, Sculptor in Ordinary to the Queen. His design called forth a storm of abuse, though it would not have been struck without the Queen's approval. In the main the public objected to the Queen being shown with a little crown perched precariously on her head, apparently ready to fall off at the slightest movement. The design as a whole contrasted badly with the previous young bare head by William Wyon. Even so the Queen did wear such a small crown on occasions and it can be seen among the Crown Jewels at the Tower.

In 1893 the coinage was again redesigned, Sir Thomas Brock producing the 'Old head' type obverse and de Saulles the reverses, save where Pistrucci's work still appeared on the gold coinage and the Crown.

Two experiments were tried with the coinage during this reign. There had long been recommendations for the introduction of a decimal coinage. Various committees had reported and some pattern pieces appeared. In 1849 the Florin, value two Shillings or one-tenth of a Pound, was put into circulation. Because the Queen's titles omitted D.G.–*Dei gratia,* by the grace of God–another storm of protest arose over the 'Godless' Florin. The design is said to have been approved by Prince Albert.

The piece was redesigned on a slightly larger flan and D.G. was included. It soon became known as the 'Gothic' Florin because of the style of design and lettering, the latter being of the old English black letter type, and because of the wave of Gothic revival that was sweeping the country. As well as the Gothic Florin a Gothic Crown was struck, on the suggestion, it is said, of the Queen. A very finely detailed bust

THE GHOST of a GUINEA or the Country Banker's Surprise!!

of the Queen paired with a design in the Gothic style on the reverse by William Dyce (1806–64), a celebrated painter, to produce a piece held by some to be Britain's most handsome coin. The issue was a small one and was, according to some accounts, immediately taken up by the bankers and by collectors. Certainly when the coin appears today it is usually in collector's condition.

Another experiment, this time unsuccessful, was the introduction of a Double Florin or Four Shilling piece. At this time the Crown was in general use and the Double Florin was so nearly the same size that the two were readily confused. The new coins were struck only for four years, from 1887 to 1890 inclusive. The same remarks

concerning similarity of size could be and were made about the Halfcrown and the Florin. In this case the former was discontinued for a number of years, from 1851 to 1873. When it reappeared the matter seems to have been forgotten and the two pieces lived together successfully till decimalization. However, one never learns from history. The main complaint about Britain's new 50 Penny piece is that it is so nearly the size of the 10 New Pence. Had it been the same size as the Halfcrown such complaints might never have arisen.

The reign of Victoria saw the first strikings in any quantity of the gold Five and Two Pound pieces. Pattern or proof pieces of either or both these denominations had been struck in very small numbers in the

206 a

206 b

207

208

209

210 a

210 b

211 a

211 b

205 *An early nineteenth-century cartoon that reflects contemporary opinion on the state of the nation's coinage. It dates from the period of the Napoleonic wars when the issue of Guineas was stopped and bank notes came into general use.*

206 a, b *George III Shilling with the laureate head, and crowned arms within the Order of the Garter on the reverse.*

207, 208, 209 *George IV Halfcrown. Pistrucci's caricature was not endured by the monarch for long, and replaced in later issues by a head based on Sir Francis Chantrey's bust, (208). (209) Reverse of the second type of Farthing of George IV.*

210 a, b *William IV Halfcrown of 1834, with the detailed draped coat-of-arms on the reverse.*

211 a, b *William IV Groat (Four Pence), issued in this reign only in 1836-7, and nicknamed a 'Joey' after Joseph Hume who suggested the revival of this coin for general circulation. The Groat of the Britannia type was again struck from 1838 till 1856. It should not be confused with the Maundy Groat which has a 4 on the reverse.*

previous three reigns and are usually to be found in specimen sets of coins put up in velvet-lined leather cases, as mentioned in Chapter I.

In dealing briefly with the coins produced since the reform of 1816 we have rather lost sight of the machines which produced them. Boulton's machines, which shook the building with the force of their blows and whose drive needed levers passing through walls and nodding high up under ceilings, were replaced in the Victorian era by Uhlhorn presses. These were quieter, since they tended to squeeze rather than strike. Dies lasted longer in them and they could strike one hundred a minute against the Boulton press's sixty. Boulton's machinery actually continued in use till about 1870-2. It is remarkable to think now that the whole work of the press room was dependent on the boxwood cogs of a single wheel. This was worn out after sixty years of use. In 1876 the wheel shed its teeth and the whole Mint was out of action for six months. By this time new machinery was being brought in and reasonable progress in this respect was maintained over the years till the move to South Wales.

Another machine which was to have very considerable influence on coinage was the reducing machine. The first of these was brought over from France and installed by Pistrucci in Wellesley-Pole's fine new mint. The authorities liked it and were soon buying another improved model. They have continued to keep pace with improvements to the machine ever since.

The reducing machine made it no longer necessary for an artist or engraver to prepare master dies for coinage in mild steel to the actual size of the coins to be struck from them. This, in the long term, made it possible for artists with no engraving experience to offer designs for coins and finally led to the suspension of the title of Chief Engraver. It has been revived in recent years. Engravers are still actively employed by the Royal Mint for medal work and for the final deft touches needed to master dies after the reducing machine has done its work.

When a design has been accepted from an artist, it is first cast in plaster of Paris on a flan of about

213 a

212 a

213 b

1889

212 b

214 a

212 c

214 b

1895

eight or ten inches in diameter. This cast is then electro-plated. The result is fitted to the tracer end of the reducing machine where, as the flan revolves, a tracing finger faithfully follows every line of the design. Through pantograph action a cutting finger at the other end of the machine cuts the design being traced on a piece of mild steel. When hardened this becomes the master punch from which dies are multiplied. The machine can reduce from the larger size almost literally to that of a pin's head.

We must now look back to 1797 for the account which was promised on the copper coinage. Here we return to Boulton and Watt and the Soho mint. The problem of small change in coins of base metal had been in existence since the time of Elizabeth I. A little had been done to meet it, notably in the reign of James I, when the Harington, Lennox and Richmond Farthings appeared. In the reign of Charles II Halfpennies and Farthings in copper, and for a short period in tin, had been minted, but the supply was never enough to meet the demand.

Part of the trouble was that the Royal Mint was not equipped to deal with a copper coinage and the problems in striking in this metal were not understood. Sir Isaac Newton, who was Warden from 1696 till 1699 and Master from 1700 till 1727, carried out a number of experiments with minting copper. He postulated that (1) coins should contain their intrinsic value of pure copper, less only the cost of making and issuing them; (2) that the entire process of coining should be undertaken by the Mint from ingots of raw metal, instead of purchasing ready-made blanks as previously; and (3) that the quantity of coin issued should be directly related to actual requirements. By so doing he hoped to provide better quality coins at a lower cost.[1]

Unfortunately, thin castings of copper proved unsound for striking coinage and the horse-driven rolling mills at the Mint were not strong enough to roll down copper ingots or thicker strip. Variations to the thickness of castings, to rolling methods and to the diameter and thickness of the copper blanks were

[1] Peck, *English Copper, Tin and Bronze Coins in the British Museum.*

212 a, b, c *Victoria Halfcrown, the obverse showing the 'Young head' and (212 b) the crowned shield reverse that was in use till 1887 when it was replaced by the 'Jubilee' square shield within the Order of the Garter (212c)*

213 a, b *The 'Jubilee' type Crown, with Pistrucci's St George and the Dragon on the reverse.*

214 a, b *The same reverse was kept for the 'Old head' Crown, struck between 1893-1900.*

215 a, b *The so-called 'Godless' Florin, struck in the Gothic style apart from the lettering but with D. G. (Dei Gratia—by the grace of God) omitted. This raised a storm of protest.*

216 a, b *The Double Florin, or Four Shilling piece, an unsuccessful experiment because the coin was too easily confused with the Crown.*

217 a, b *Victorian Farthing of 1873, with a youthful bust of the Queen, and Britannia seated between the ship and the lighthouse.*

215 a

215 b

217 a

217 b

216 a

216 b

all tried by Newton. The results look excellent, but when the coins were heated and hammered—a primitive process known as the 'hammer test'—they split. Newton concluded that tin had been added to the copper, against orders. The Mint went back to buying copper strip already rolled down to the correct thickness for coin blanks.

Towards the end of the eighteenth century, as we have seen, Boulton's Soho mint came into operation. He had struck token pieces and had undertaken a coinage for the East India Company. He campaigned for a proper copper coinage, in much the same terms as Newton, and in 1797 was given a contract to provide such a coinage.

This contract produced the large two-ounce Twopence and the one-ounce Penny which, by reason of their thick rims, were at once given the name of 'cartwheels'. The Twopence was struck only in 1797. It was too big and heavy to find favour but, true to the Newton/Boulton requirements, it was so accurate in weight that it could be, and for a long period often was, used as a two-ounce weight on a pair of scales.

Unfortunately no sooner had this coinage been produced than the price of copper rose sharply. There

was at once more than a pennyworth of copper in a Penny. The whole design, lightened in weight, without the Twopence but with a Farthing, was struck again in the period 1799–1807, after which copper coinage lapsed till 1821. By its resumption the new Mint was in operation and equipped to deal with this metal.

Coinage continued to be struck in copper, though it was always reasonably expensive, until 1860. By that time the rather large pieces were being frowned on and it was decided to issue base metal coinage in bronze for the future. L. C. Wyon produced a version of his 'Young head' of the Queen for the obverse in the form of a bust. He also produced his well-liked reverse with Britannia, seated right, upon a rock with a lighthouse and ship to left and right. The reducing machine obligingly provided smaller versions of the design for the Halfpenny and Farthing.

There was no 'Jubilee head' bronze coinage, the next change being to Brock's 'Old head' type. De Saulles modified the reverse design, omitting the lighthouse and ship. The latter never returned, while the former reappeared in 1937 and remained till the end of the series.

THE COIN TODAY

The fairly short reign of Edward VII (1901–10) saw some modification in the designs of the coinage but no additional or experimental pieces were added to the range. The Crown appeared only in 1902, with the St George reverse. The Florin was now firmly established and on this piece de Saulles (1862–1903), Chief Engraver at the Royal Mint, achieved a design which met with considerable approval. It showed Britannia, with trident and shield, standing on the prow of a ship. This was something new to British coinage and was in part based on a somewhat similar design, but without the ship's prow, which the same artist had used on the British Dollar. This was a handsome Crown size silver piece which had first appeared in 1895 for use in the Far East. In this instance there was a complete ship in the left background. De Saulles' use of the crest of the Royal Arms, a lion standing on a crown, on the Shilling also seems generally to have been approved. It continued in use during the next reign, George V's (1910–36), was modified in 1927 and was also used on the Sixpence from 1911 to 1927.

Several interesting things happened to the coinage during George V's reign. The first came as a shock to collectors. When the new coinage appeared in 1911 there was no Crown. This caused some protests and after representations had been made by the eminent numismatic societies the piece finally made its appearance in 1927 as a proof included in the specimen sets and as a circulation piece in 1928. Even so the numbers struck were extremely small, making every year between 1928 and 1936, save only 1935, a rarity. In that year the Jubilee of the King was celebrated, and a Crown, the reverse designed by Percy Metcalfe, was struck in commemoration. The artist's

'mechanical man' rendering of the St George and the dragon motif caused considerable adverse comment.

The next event of interest was the lowering of the standard of the silver coinage in 1920 for the first time in four hundred years. This was caused by the rise in the price of silver. The metal received a fifty-per-cent alloy of nickel, which at first proved unsatisfactory, the coins wearing and discolouring badly. This was later rectified and the public soon forgot the matter.

Finally, no gold coins were issued after 1917, except for a recoinage of Sovereigns in 1925 undertaken for technical reasons. Though Sovereigns of the same high standard as those first struck in the reign of George III reappeared in the reign of Elizabeth II they were not struck for circulation.

The reign of George VI (1937–52) commenced with the silver coinage still being struck with the fifty-per-cent alloy – 500 fine in technical terms. This was to last till 1946. As a result of the Second World War and of the large amount of actual silver which Britain had to repay to the United States, silver coinage was then abolished and cupro-nickel took its place. The four little Maundy coins were, however, upgraded to 925 fine silver, the fineness in use till 1925, and so continue to be struck.

The effect of this measure was that the coins now put into use had virtually no intrinsic value. We have already seen something of the many struggles to issue a coinage whose pieces contained their value in the metal of which they were made. The economy of Britain and many other countries has been frequently shaken over the centuries by the issue of undervalued and debased coins. Now, in 1947, all pretence at intrinsic value was cast aside, 'silver' coins were issued in base metal,

218 a, b *Edward VII Florin, a coin that became even more firmly established with de Saulles' popular Britannia design on the reverse.*

218 a

219 a, b *George V Crown, 1932. No Crown appeared in George V's reign until 1927, and thereafter they were struck in very limited numbers except for 1935. This coin is therefore a rarity.*

220 *The crowned numeral was on the reverse of the silver Threepence until it was redesigned in 1927. The Maundy Threepence, however, still retained the crowned 3.*

218 b

ONE FLORIN · TWO SHILLINGS
1903

valued at only a few pence when compared with the stated value of the coins, and thus Britain's money became nothing more than tokens.

Money, say the economists, is a promise to pay. The coins circulating now are only the promise of a promise. Britain was not alone in the issue of token money. Those who travelled abroad even before the Second World War were frequently struck by the poor quality and lightness in weight of base metal coins which they received in various parts of Europe. Now, however, Britain fell into line, though it is to the credit of the Treasury that the coins issued in cupro-nickel, though worthless, still had a good weight and a solid feel. They are not yet reduced to such wretched, light, insubstantial token pieces as one finds in use in so many European countries. Even so at this moment a crisis in the nickel market could cause some rethinking about the new decimal coinage, just coming into use, though the recent find of large nickel deposits in Australia may stabilize the situation. It would be ironic if, at the very moment when Britain is trying to supplant the paper 10s note with a cupro-nickel 50 Penny piece, a shortage of nickel and a sharp rise in price should make this impossible.

Since 1947 even the countries where gold and silver are mined— South Africa, Australia, the United States, as well as others—have gradually had to lower the standards of the coinage by the increase in the use of base metal coins. It is only fair to point out that the rise in the price of silver, though partly caused by the aftermath of World War, is also partly caused by ever-increasing demands for the metal by industry, demands such that the supply will scarcely meet them. One example of this is the enormous growth of photography, not only by the increase in interest by the man-in-

219 a

GEORGIVS V DEI GRA: BRITT: OMN: REX

220

219 b

221, 222 *The new Royal Mint at Llantrisant. (221) shows a general view of the coining presses, which have an automatic blank feed system from above and a coin 'take-off' conveyor. Each press produces between 200-250 coins per minute. (222) shows the electronic counting and bagging machines.*

the-street—who now rarely moves unless festooned with photographic apparatus—but in industry and medicine and many other fields. Photography absorbs large quantities of nitrate of silver and makes its contribution to the rise in price.

Something was said in earlier chapters of the moving of the Royal Mint from the Tower and of the new machinery which was installed to produce the coinage. In 1968 the Queen opened an entirely new Royal Mint at Talbot Green, Llantrisant, Glamorgan, and the work of transferring the production of money began to move from Little Tower Hill.

The new Mint was constructed to produce the great quantity of coinage which will be needed to replace the present British denominations when the whole range of decimal money comes into use in 1971. Meanwhile the London Mint is being gradually run down and will finally be vacated. It is said that the fine original buildings will remain but that the others will be demolished and the site redeveloped.

The use to which Smirke's building will be put has not yet been stated. It would appear to offer itself as a museum for the fine collection of dies, seals, coins and medals which the Royal Mint possesses and which so few of the public are ever privileged to see. The Royal Mint collection covers far more ground than just the modern coins which have been struck at the present location since 1816. With the British Museum

crying out for more space perhaps it might be possible for the two government departments to amalgamate, the two collections to be put together and housed and displayed in a British Museum Numismatic Centre, just as Natural History is dealt with at South Kensington. There would then be no finer collection of coins nor a better numismatic centre in the world. The two learned numismatic Societies, the Royal and the British, both of which are tenants in other owners' property, might be afforded facilities for meetings and library housing, thus making a complete numismatic unit in Britain, a unit which scholars and visitors alike would travel the world to see.

In the meantime the new Mint at Llantrisant has been declared by one who has visited many of the world's mints to be the finest of them all. We saw something of the primitive automation introduced by Boulton. He was, in fact, one of the fathers of time-and-motion studies in that he tried to plan his mint as well as his factory at Soho in such a way that time and effort were not wasted by the ill-location of the various machines and processes in relation to each other. To time-and-motion there has now been added automation and full advantage of both has been taken in the building and equipping of the new Mint. Only two men are needed to programme the operation of the entire handling system by which the blanks pass through their various

223

224

225 a

225 b

223   *1962 Penny.*

224   *Threepenny piece with the three flowers of the thrift plant on the reverse.*

225 a, b   *Commemorative Crown struck on the Coronation of the Queen, 1953.*

226   *George VI Sixpence, with the reverse showing a crown over the initials GRI. From 1949-52 these initials became GRVI.*

227   *George VI 'English' Shilling, as opposed to the 'Scottish' Shilling which had a lion seated on the crown and holding a Sword and Sceptre. Both 'lion on crown' motifs are the crest of the Royal Arms of the respective countries.*

228   *Reverse of George V Florin, showing the cruciform sceptres with a shield in each angle.*

processes and are finally passed to the coining machines. Three twin lines of presses, with fourteen presses in each line, strike the various denominations at rates of up to three hundred a minute – a far cry from Boulton's sixty-a-minute machines. All the other processes are linked to keep up with this flow, so that the millions of coins needed to keep Britain supplied with money can be produced.

So far as modern British coins are concerned their whole history since 1870 can be traced by the study of the Annual Report of the Deputy Master and Comptroller of the Royal Mint. These Reports were instituted in 1870, and saw their centenary in 1969. Each year's Report covers the entire work of the Royal Mint in all its many phases.

What is of particular interest to the collector is, naturally, the statement of the numbers of each denomination of coin struck during the year. These lists cover not only the coins struck for Britain but for the one-time Colonies, the members of the present Commonwealth of Nations and for the many foreign countries which have their coins struck under contract at the British Royal Mint.

Throughout the century a tremendous amount of information on the whole subject of coinage will be found. Experiments with metals, trials of new substances such as aluminium when it became available, the work of the branch mints over their period of connection with Tower Hill, the striking of awards and commemorative medals, discussions on coin designs, Royal Proclamations of new coinages: these and a host of other subjects are dealt with in the Reports.

Thus we have seen something of the coin today. On a global basis millions of millions are needed, in spite of paper money, credit cards, cheques and the like. For example,

one of the first tasks of the new Royal Mint was to produce sufficient of the new decimal denominations of Two, One and Half New Pence to replace the five thousand million Pennies, Threepences and Sixpences which it is estimated will be in circulation on the day they are superseded by the new money – and this in Britain alone.

We have covered a large span of time since we first started to look at coins in the earlier chapters. Now that the end of the story has been reached it is hoped that what has been written will prove to be of interest to both student-collector and investor-collector alike. There are few subjects that open up wider fields of interest than that of numismatics.

226

227

228

229 *Britain's new decimal currency. The reverse side of the coins was designed by Christopher Ironside, and the Royal portrait common to the obverse side of all of them was engraved by Arnold Machin.*

230 *The Queen opened the new Royal Mint at Llantrisant, Glamorgan, in December 1968. This view shows the exterior of the coining block.*

Glossary, *Places to Visit and Further Reading*

Descriptions of coin condition

FDC = Fleur-de-coin; flawless, without any wear or damage. With a hammered coin, probably with a 'fleur' or patina of age.

Unc. = Uncirculated. Used with reference to modern coins which, though straight from the mint, will have slight damage due to minting methods. Has never circulated.

EF = Extremely fine. With very little sign of wear or of having been in circulation.

VF = Very fine. Allows of slight signs of wear. Should be replaced by a better specimen if possible.

F = Fine. With fairly considerable signs of wear. Should be replaced by a better specimen if possible.

Fair = Very considerably worn.

Poor = Of no value as a collector's piece unless of great rarity.

The above may sometimes be used together, as:

EF–VF = Condition falls between the two.

EF/VF = Obverse EF, reverse VF.

Metals

AV = Gold.
AR = Silver.
Æ = Copper or bronze.
Cu–ni. = Cupro-nickel.
Al. = Aluminium.
Other metals, such as lead, pewter, usually given in full.

Rarity

Used with ancient coins:
RRRR = Highest rarity.
RRR = Extremely rare.
RR = Very rare.
R = Rare.
S = Scarce.
Used with more modern coins:
R7 = Only one or two known.
R6 = Three or four known.
R5 = Five to ten known.
R4 = Eleven to twenty known.
R3 = Extremely rare.
R2 = Very rare.
R = Rare.
S = Scarce.
N = Normal, neither scarce nor common.
C = Common.
C2 = Very common.
C3 = Extremely common.
Devised by Wilson Peck for use with copper and bronze:
EXC = Excessively common.
EC = Extremely common.
VC = Very common.
C = Common.
S = Scarce.
VS = Very scarce.
R = Rare.
VR = Very rare.
ER = Extremely rare.
EXR = Excessively rare.
PU = Probably unique.

Some definitions

BLANK – the flan before it has been struck into a coin.

BROCKAGE – a coin with the design in relief on one side and the same design incuse on the other. Caused by a struck coin sticking in the machine, a further blank being fed in and the first coin acting as a 'die'. A brockage may be of either obverse or reverse.

DEVICE or TYPE – the main design, e.g. St George and the dragon, shield of arms, etc.

EXERGUE – a small section usually at the lower part of a coin and divided from the design by a line, the space so formed usually occupied by the date; cf. a normal British Penny, pre-decimalization.

FIELD – the main part of the flan on which the design or device appears.

FLAN or PLANCHET – the circular or otherwise shaped piece of metal forming the body of the coin.

LEGEND – the lettering or inscription on the coin.

MINT – the place at which coins are normally struck, such as the Royal Mint.

MINT MARK – a symbol used to show the place of minting, the date of minting, or both, or the person by whom the coin was struck or for whom it was struck. Sometimes used to show the source of metal: example, a plume of feathers on an English hammered coin sometimes designates silver from Welsh mines.

MONEYER – the person responsible for striking a coin. His name frequently appeared on Anglo-Saxon, Norman and later Pennies.

MULE – a coin struck from two dies which are not properly used together; example, a coin with the obverse of a Jersey Penny and the reverse of a British Penny.

OBVERSE – the side usually showing the monarch's head.

PATTERN – a coin struck to a suggested design but not eventually put into circulation. Usually struck with a brilliant finish and in FDC condition.

PROOF – a coin struck specially from polished dies on a polished flan of a type or design of coin which is used in circulation.

REVERSE – the back or opposite side to the obverse.

Mint marks

There are about 126 different mint marks on English hammered coins, of which the following are examples:

Animals and Birds
Boar's head
Dragon
Greyhound's head
Leopard's head
Lion
Lion rampant
Martlet
Ostrich's head
Swan

Fruits and Flowers
Acorn
Eglantine

Flower and B (Briot's mark)
Gerbe (wheatsheaf)
Grapes
Leaf
Pansy
Pear
Pinecone
Pomegranate
Rose
Rosette
Thistle
Trefoil (clover leaf)

Miscellaneous
A
Anchor
Arrow
Bell
Book
Bow
Br (Bristol)
Cardinal's hat
Castle
Catherine-wheel
Coronet
Cross (about 21 varieties)
Crown
Crozier (cross-bearer)
Eye
Grapple
Hand
Harp
Heart
Key
(P)
Plume of feathers
(R)
Sceptre
Sun
Sword
Woolpack
Y

Museums where coins may be seen and where important collections exist

Britain
Ashmolean Museum, Oxford
Bristol, City Museum
The British Museum
Chester, Grosvenor Museum
Devizes Museum

Fitzwilliam Museum, Cambridge
Huddersfield, Tolson Memorial Museum
Hunterian Museum, Glasgow
Leeds, City Museum
Lincoln, City and County Museum
Maidstone, Museum and Art Gallery
Manchester Museum
Newark-on-Trent Museum
Newcastle-upon-Tyne, Black Gate Museum
Sheffield Museum
Shrewsbury Museum
Southampton, Tudor House Museum
Sunderland Museum
Winchester, City Museum
York, the Yorkshire Museum

Europe
Cabinet des Médailles, Bibliothèque Nationale, Paris
Le Musée de la Monnaie, Paris
Cabinet des Médailles, Bibliothèque Royale, Brussels
Mint Museum, Utrecht
Royal Coin Cabinet, The Hague
Royal Danish Coin & Medal Collection, Copenhagen
University Coin Cabinet, Oslo
Royal Coin Cabinet, Stockholm
Hamburg Historical Museum, Hamburg
Swiss National Museum, Zurich
Archaeological Museum, Madrid
The Mint, Lisbon
National Museum, Rome
The Vatican Collection, Rome
Federal Coin Cabinet, Vienna
National Museum, Prague
National Museum, Sofia
National Museum, Belgrade
National Magyar Museum, Budapest
National Museum of Antiquities, Bucharest
National Coin Cabinet, Athens
National Collection, Istanbul
National Museum, Helsinki
National Museum, Warsaw
Hermitage Museum, Leningrad
Moscow Art Museum

North America
Metropolitan Museum of Art, New York
Museum of the American Numismatic Society, New York
Princeton Library, Princeton, New York
Dumbarton Oaks Collection, Washington, D.C.
Smithsonian Institution, Washington, D.C.
Museum of Fine Arts, Boston
Fogg Art Museum, Harvard University, Cambridge, Mass.
Yale Collection, New Haven, Conn.
U.S. Mint Museum, Philadelphia
The Cleveland Museum of Art, Cleveland
Seattle Art Museum, Seattle, Washington

(The above are only a selection.)

Coin auctioneers holding regular sales
Christie, Manson & Woods, King Street, London, S.W.1.
Glendining & Co. Ltd., Blenheim Street, New Bond Street, London, W.1.
Sotheby & Co., New Bond Street, London, W.1.
Wallis & Wallis, High Street, Lewes, Sussex
J. Schulman, Kaisersgracht 448, Amsterdam, Netherlands
Hotel Drouot, Paris
Munzen und Medaillen, Basle

Many other auctioneers hold coin sales but the above specialize in this type of sale.

Periodicals dealing with coins and coin collecting
The Australian Coin Review, by Hawthorn Press, Melbourne
The British Numismatic Journal, annually, by the British Numismatic Society
Canadian Numismatic Journal, by the Canadian Numismatic Society, Ottawa

The *Coin and Medal Bulletin,*
monthly, by B.A. Seaby, Ltd.,
London
Coins, monthly, by Link House
Group, Croydon, Surrey
Coins, Medals and Currency,
weekly, by Morland Lee, Ltd.,
London
Coin World, from Sidney, Ohio,
U.S.A.
*Journal of the Token & Medal
Society,* from Sidney, Ohio
New Zealand Numismatic Journal,
from Wellington, New Zealand
The *Numismatic Chronicle,* annually,
by the Royal Numismatic Society
The *Numismatic Circular,* monthly,
by Spink & Son, London
The *Numismatic Gazette,* by
Corbitt & Hunter, Newcastle-
upon-Tyne
Numismatic Scrapbook Magazine,
from Chicago, Ill., U.S.A.
The *Numismatist,* from the
American Numismatic Association

(The above are only a selection.)

Books of general interest on the whole subject

Greek
HEAD, B. V. *A Guide to the
Principal Coins of the Greeks*
HEAD, B. V. *Historia Numorum.
A manual of Greek Numismatics*
SEABY *Greek Coins and their
Values*
SELTMAN, C. T. *Greek Coins*

Roman and Byzantine
GOODACRE, H. *A Handbook of the
Coinage of the Byzantine Empire*
MATTINGLY, H. *Roman Coins,
from the earliest times to the fall of
the Western Empire*
SEAR, D. R. *Roman Coins and their
Values*

General
ALLEN, J. J. Cullimore *The History
of the British Sovereign*
BRESSET, K. E. *A Guide Book of*

English Coins
BROOKE, G. C. *English Coins*
CARSON, R. A. G. *Coins, Ancient,
Mediaeval and Modern*
CHARLTON, J. E. *Standard
Catalogue of Canadian Coins,
Tokens and Paper Money*
CLARKE, R. L. *Catalog of the
Coins of British Oceania*
COOLE, A. B. *Coins in China's
History*
CRAIG, W. D. *Coins of the World,
1750–1850*
DAVENPORT, J. *European Crowns,
1700–1800*
DAVENPORT, J. *European
Crowns and Talers since 1800*
DAVENPORT, J. *German Talers,
1700–1800*
DOWLE, A. and FINN, P. *The
Guide Book to the Coinage of
Ireland, from 995* AD *to the present
day*
FRIEDBERG, R. *Coins of the
British World, complete from 500* AD
to the present
FRIEDBERG, R. *Gold Coins of the
World, complete from 600* AD *to 1958*
SOMER JAMES *The Guide Book
of Canadian Coins, Currency and
Tokens*
LE MAY *The Coinage of Siam*
LINECAR, H. W. A. *The Crown
Pieces of Great Britain and the
British Commonwealth*
LINECAR, H. W. A. *The Milled
Coinage of England, 1662–1946*
LINECAR, H. W. A. and STONE,
A. G. *English Proof and Pattern
Crown Size Pieces*
MACK, R. P. *The Coinage of
Ancient Britain*
NORTH, J. J. *English Hammered
Coinage.* Two volumes
PRIDMORE, F. *The Coins of the
British Commonwealth of Nations to
the end of the reign of George VI,
1952.* Three volumes; more in
preparation
WAYTE RAYMOND *The Silver
Dollars of North and South America*
REMICK, J. and SOMER JAMES
The Guide Book and Catalogue of

*British Commonwealth Coins,
1660–1969*
SEABY, B. A. Ltd. *Standard
Catalogue of British Coins*
SEABY P. J. and MONICA
BUSSELL *British Copper Coins and
their Values*
SHAW, Miss E. M. *A History of
Currency in South Africa*
STEWART, I. H. *The Scottish
Coinage*
YEOMAN, R. S. *Catalogue of
Modern World Coins, 1850–1964*
YEOMAN, R. S. *A Guide Book of
United States Coins*

War medals and decorations
JOSLIN, E. C. *The Standard
Catalogue of British Orders,
Decorations and Medals*

An annual bibliographical list of all
current and standard works on
every phase of coin and medal
collecting, entitled 'About Those
Coins', is published by Spink &
Son, London; free on request.

Index

Acknowledgments

American Numismatic Society
Australian News and Information
    Bureau
Bibliothèque Nationale
Brown Brothers
Central Office of Information
Culver Pictures
John Freeman Ltd.
Ray Gardner
Terry Hardy
Michael Holford
Mansell Collection
National Archaeological Museum,
    Athens
New Zealand Treasury
The Oriental Institute, University
    of Chicago
Sandhill Imports
Science Museum
Sotheby & Co.
Spink & Son, Ltd.
Trustees of the British Museum